The Beat

KEVIN BEATTIE

with
Neal Manning

Skript Design & Publishing

The Beat

Published by Skript Design & Publishing, 26 Harebell Drive, Witham, Essex CM8 2XB

British Library Cataloguing-in-Publication Data
A catalogue record for this book is available from the British Library.
ISBN 1-874799-08-3

Typeset in 9/10pt Palatino by Skript Design & Publishing

Printed and bound in Great Britain by
St Edmundsbury Press, Bury St Edmunds, Suffolk IP33 3TU

Contents

ACKNOWLEDGEMENTS

MAIN SPONSORS:
Roger K Day, Archway Events, Phoenix Properties (Ipswich) Ltd
Michael Smith, Michael Smith & Co, Solicitors, Ipswich
Langford Pearce Developments Ltd.
Alan James, Jayrest, Hadleigh

There are a few people I would now like to thank for their assistance throughout the completion of the book:

John & Kay Cox, Aston Car Sales, Ipswich
Bob Williams, The Salutation, Ipswich
Kevin, Belstead Arms, Ipswich
Shirley & Paul Bendall, The Selkirk, Ipswich
Herbie Went, A & R Builders, Ipswich
Malcolm Roberts, East Anglian Fruit and Veg Limited
Dave Ashford, Rose & Crown, Elmsett
Ron Mann, The Copy Centre, Ipswich
Peter Barnes, The Bed Factory, Ipswich
Chantry News, Ipswich
The Orchard & Top Cuts, Ipswich
Dave, The Haven, Ipswich
Graham Plumbley, Barkers Community Store, Ipswich
Lees Kitchen, Ipswich
Dominique, The Spinning Wheel, Hadleigh
Jarnie, The Eight Bells, Hadleigh
Bob Spall Construction, Ipswich
Jason Dozzell, ex Ipswich Town F.C.
Alan Haste, Avon Crown Limited, Ipswich
Tony Armstrong, BAP Transport, Colchester
Ken Bean, The Chev Club, Ipswich
Ray Smith, Bit Conservancing, Ipswich
Graham Emmerson, SEH Windows and Doors, Ipswich
Terry and Rita Butcher, The Old Manor Hotel, Stirling
David Sadler, Carter Sadler, Ipswich
Adrian Holmes, Sun Bed Hire, Ipswich
Ralph, Retone East Anglia Limited
the late Frank Rigby, Dental Surgeon, Ipswich
Alan, Lambourne Clothing, Ipswich

The Beat

John Stringer, HTL Transport Limited, Felixstowe
Globeright Limited, Ipswich
Tony Taylor, Taylors Pet Supplies, Newmarket
Dean, Ketley Asphalt, Chelmsford
Nick Charles, Ipswich
Premier Pool Centre, Ipswich
GJ Spurdens Newsagents, Ipswich
O.B.O. Scaffolding, Ipswich
J.Pooley, Ipswich
Roger Woshalo, Car Glass and Trim Ipswich Limited
Frank Howard, Westerfield House, Ipswich
John & Graeme Keeble, Bramford, Ipswich
Ian Dennison, Ipswich
Kuda Limited, Ipswich
Hughie Bell, The Health Centre, Carlisle
Frank Peacock, Fruit and Veg, Colchester
Brian and Sandra Peat, Q Marketing, Preston, Lancs
Danny, Elm Garage, Ipswich
Ray Smith, Bit Con Surfacing, Ipswich
Garneys & Hill, Ipswich
Barry Dye Entertainments
Hermtune – Brian Offord & family
Maggie & Phil Mann
Jeff's Cafe, Ipswich
The Pack family, Eastern Structures Limited
Brian, West End Carpets
Alby Kingham, C,C-S Dry Cleaning

PICTURE ACKNOWLEDGEMENTS

The photographs in this book are reproduced by
kind permission of the following:

Ken Carpenter
Owen Hines
East Anglian Daily Times
Sporting Pictures Limited
The Evening Star
Coloursport
The Press Association

For Maggie, Emma, Sarah, and Louise,
with love.

NEAL MANNING

NEAL MANNING has worked for the East Anglian Daily Times Co Ltd since 1960 and on it's sister papers, The Evening Star and Green 'Un, the Saturday night football paper, apart from a year when he lived in Canada.

For many years he covered the fortunes of Ipswich Town both at home and abroad, including the glory days of the club under Bobby Robson. In 1981, the year the Town won the UEFA Cup, he covered all sixty-six matches that the club played in their quest for the Football League Championship and the F.A. Cup which they came so close to winning. In the end they had to settle for lifting the UEFA Cup on an unforgettable night in Amsterdam.

Neal also had the privilege of following Kevin Beattie's career which certainly had its highs and lows. "The Beat" at his best was an outstanding player and it was a pity that injury was to cut short his career.

A keen sportsman himself, Neal still plays cricket and golf on a regular basis, and from a work point of view covers the local scene whether it be football, golf, rugby or bowls.

Neal lives with his partner, Debbie, and has two boys, Robert and John, who both live and work locally.

Foreword
by John Motson

Football is full of hard-luck stories, but there are few to compare with that of Kevin Beattie.

Kevin was special, a colossus of a player who never fulfiled his potential – and whose career was eventually curtailed – as he fought in vain to overcome a succession of injury problems.

As an emerging talent in the early 70's, Kevin's impact was considerable and soon comparisons were being made with the late, great Duncan Edwards. Praise indeed. His club manager, Bobby Robson, maintains to this day that Beattie was the nearest thing he had seen to the outstanding young Manchester United player who so tragically lost his life in the Munich Air Disaster.

And Bobby, as shrewd a judge of a footballer as you are likely to find, also insists Kevin should have gone on to win a record number of England caps in the position which World Cup-winning captain, Bobby Moore, made his own for so long.

Instead, by the time his club manager had taken over the national reins, Kevin had been forced into retirement, with a mere nine caps to his credit.

I have several abiding memories of Kevin, concerning his contrasting fortunes on the field of play, the slightly madcap side to his character and the illness problems that were to blight him later in life.

I remember his headed goal for England in their 5-1 demolition of Scotland at Wembley in 1975, when it seemed he could look forward to so many similar highs at the peak of his profession.

I recall, too, how he fractured his arm in an F.A. Cup semi-final against Manchester City at Villa Park six years later, which in a way signalled the beginning of the end. On a humourous note, I will never forget covering a pre-Christmas fixture at

Portman Road for Match of the Day and I found myself in the dressing-room area awaiting confirmation of the team line-ups.

Kevin, ever-willing, had agreed to dress up as Father Christmas for a club promotion that had, for some reason, been delayed.

An anxious-looking Bobby Robson emerged from the home dressing room at 2.30pm to tell me: "I've got a big game in half an hour and my centre-half is running around dressed up as Santa Claus!".

That was typical of Kevin, as was the determination he displayed when struck down by pancreatitis. I called in to the hospital, only to be told he was not well enough to have visitors, and I am delighted that he went on to make such a good recovery.

At the height of his career, Kevin displayed searing pace, incredible athleticism and sheer physical strength that set him apart from his contemporaries as a genuinely world-class talent.

One of Kevin's most endearing qualities is that he bears no grudges and displays no bitterness that his earning potential, even if he had prolonged his time in football, was way short of today's highly-paid stars.

It is also to his eternal credit that he has always made light of his problems, and I trust those supporters with fond recollections of Kevin's career will enjoy the trip down memory lane that this book provides.

John Motson
Harpenden
May, 1998.

1

The Diamond

Bobby Robson called me his Diamond soon after I had made my first team debut for Ipswich Town in August 1972.

It was a nickname that was to stick with me for several years, but by the end of my career at Portman Road, which had been cut short by injury, the Diamond had definitely lost its sparkle.

Bobby Robson said recently that he would bracket me in a list of Britain's all-time best players – names like Stanley Matthews, Tom Finney, Bobby Charlton, Duncan Edwards, Wilf Mannion, Len Shackleton, Bryan Robson and George Best – what a great accolade from my former boss.

It got to a stage that I thought I may as well have my own nameplate on one of the treatment tables. It was getting me down having to go through the same routine week in and week out. I hated being injured and, instead of training with the rest of the players, I spent the time lying on the treatment table.

Call me naive, but I just loved playing football and I never imagined for a moment what the long term effects might be.

I had more pinpricks in my knee than a News of the World dartboard and although injections got me through games, I was in agony afterwards. My knee used to blow up like a balloon and I could not walk properly for a couple of days after a game. All the time I was having the injections I thought they were helping me.

It is true that the jabs did not affect my performance but it meant I was on the treatment table for most of the week before and after games.

It was only after I had seen David Dandy, the eminent surgeon in Cambridge, that the full picture emerged. Mr Dandy was the pioneer of keyhole surgery and many great sportsmen, including England World Cup captain Alan Shearer and current

Ipswich Town manager George Burley, have benefited from his expertise.

Mr Dandy had first seen me on June 12th, 1980 when he had arranged to look inside my knee.

In a letter to my agent, Mark Lomas, Mr Dandy wrote:

"He then had scar tissue in the joint, which I cut, and he did very well at first, but I did note that he had quite severe damage on the joint surfaces and it was clear that the knee was going to shorten his career substantially."

"It was certainly among the worst I have seen in a patient of that age and certainly the most distressing in view of the skills that would be lost to British football because of the damage in his joint."

"Sadly, Kevin's story is not unusual. Patients who have their cartilages out after tearing a ligament in the knee develop degenerative osteoarthritis very rapidly and cannot continue with their career."

"The problem is perhaps treated better now than it was twenty years ago, but there are still many players following Kevin's path after knee injuries."

I remember the year before I first saw Mr Dandy. We were due to play Barcelona in the European Cup Winners' Cup third round with the first leg at Portman Road.

I had recently had a cartilage operation on my right knee and the game against the Spanish giants was just nine days later. Robson was desperate for me to play in this massive cup-tie.

"Are you fit to play Beat?", Robson asked.

"No", I said. As far as I was concerned it was too great a risk and far too soon to play in such an important game.

I had also taken advice from the doctor at the old Ipswich Hospital in Angelsea Road who told me that there could be serious repercussions if I played.

However, as far as I was concerned that was great advice that he gave me and I did not play. We won the first game 2-1 and went down to Barcelona 1- 0 in Spain two weeks later and went out on the away goal rule.

The knee trouble itself started back in November 1975 when I played for England against Portugal in the European

Championship qualifier in Lisbon. We drew 1-1 and I can remember getting a kick and twisting my knee which at the time I thought nothing about and was able to finish the match O.K.

I went back to Ipswich and was diagnosed as having cartilage trouble.

Ipswich were having a good season and Bobby Robson said that we could win the First Division Championship, something he had set his heart on winning. Winning the title is every manager's dream.

I could only train on a very limited basis during the week. Eventually I had to have an operation, but I was soon up and about running and when the following season came I thought my problems were over. Halfway through the season my knee started playing up again and it was back to the jabs and the treatment table.

I did not think it right that the physiotherapist should be giving players injections and I believe that that was a job for the doctor only.

My other cartilage started to play me up the following season. We played West Bromwich Albion and Cyrille Regis caught me on the side the knee and it blew up like a melon. I was on sticks for two weeks. I had the fluid drained off and a jab so I could play and I did have to miss one game because they could not get enough fluid out of the knee.

The trouble would not go away so I went to Cambridge to see a specialist, who was not Mr Dandy, and this chap opened up the knee and found ligament damage. He said he sorted it out and put me in plaster from thigh to toe. Two days after getting home, blood was coming through the plaster and I went to hospital and they cut a window in the plaster and what a bloody sight it was. You could see my bone and there was a bloody big hole that should not have been there. They found out that the stitches had been put in the wrong way round. The ones that dissolve should have been inside and the other ones on the outside.

For two weeks I had to go to a local hospital to have cotton wool put into the wound to try and close the gap. Then the club's medical staff recommended that they should send me to

11

a rehabilitation centre in Slough for five months. I went to Slough driving up on the Monday morning and coming back on the Friday night. This was not a place for sports injuries which I found strange at the time.

There were labourers, bin men, bricklayers and if you call that specialist treatment for sports injuries then my name is King Tut. I was pissed off with Slough because I was not getting the right treatment and I was glad to get out of the place.

By the way the surgeon who had put the stitches in the wrong way round was only there once a day and you want to see the bloody scar he has left on my right knee and he said there should be no scar left there at all!

If only I had seen Mr Dandy when my problems first started, I am convinced would have played until I was at least forty and got a hundred caps for England instead of all those jabs and tablets they gave me for trying to keep the swelling down.

My final game for Ipswich was against Manchester City in the semi-final of the F.A. Cup and we were all over them, but I didn't finish the game. I broke my arm going for a header and the lad who I was going up against headed my arm and broke it. I can honestly say that if I had stayed on we would have beaten them in the end. They won 1-0 and then lost to Spurs in the final.

Then came the day I had to see Mr Dandy and it came as no surprise that he said I would have to give the game up at the top level. I can say now I cried and what really pissed me off was that I had to go and see Mr Dandy myself. When I got back to the Gaffer's office he said,

"I thought you would have to quit".

Then the Chairman came in and was choked but said,

"Don't worry son, there will be a job somewhere for you at this club".

Two months before Mr Dandy told me I had to quit, Coventry City came in for me. Gordon Milne was the boss and looking back I was weeks away from going on the scrap heap and Ipswich didn't even want to sell me. Even more illogical from my point of view was Ipswich's decision not to allow me to go to Norwich City soon after I had left them.

Ken Brown was the boss at the Canaries and a very nice chap who knew of my injury problems but still wanted me to go to Norwich. Ken was happy with what he had seen and wanted me at the club. Then on the Friday he came up to me and said,

"I am so sorry Beat, but the chairman won't let me have you".

He was sick I could tell.

I suppose the chairman of Town, Mr John Cobbold and Mr Arthur South of Norwich City had come to some sort of agreement that I couldn't play for Norwich. The funny thing is that I could go to Colchester with big Allan Hunter and there I met a great guy called Charlie Simpson, the physiotherapist who got me running differently and this certainly helped me to play on a lot longer.

Every morning he would take me out onto the pitch and watch me run. This went on for a couple of days and then he said,

"I have it, when you run, your feet seem to stick out. Why don't you try turning them in a little bit?".

It was hard, but after getting the knack the way I was running took all the pressures off my ligaments so my knee would not swell up after a game.

The guy was a great physio and he is sadly missed by his death. I only played three games for Colchester United and then I went to Middlesbrough which is thanks to Charlie. I will never forget what he did for me.

Cheers mate.

So then I moved off to Middlesbrough where Malcolm Allison was the manager at Ayresome Park and what a year I was to have under him.

2

Bobby Robson

The first time I met Bobby Robson was on the Monday morning after I had made my debut for the Youth team at Fulham. What sticks out in my mind is that he made me feel so welcome. For the first six months at Portman Road I didn't see much of the Gaffer as I trained and played for the Youth team which was run by Roy McCrohan, but one early memory was of Mr Robson and, his coach, Cyril Lea each giving me a shirt. When I first arrived in Ipswich I had not got a penny and very little clothing. Being one of a large family my parents simply could not afford to clothe us all properly. The club rules were that each player had to wear a collar and tie when we travelled to a match. Mr Robson realised I had a problem and that is why he and Cyril each gave me a shirt and a couple of ties for good measure.

Although the Gaffer's main responsibility was the first team, he always kept an eye on the club as a whole. From time to time he would come and see us and ask us if we had any problems. At one time I told him that I was unhappy with my digs, so he told me to go home to Carlisle for a fortnight with a promise that on my return he would have sorted out new digs for me. He was as good as his word and I was much happier after that.

It did not take long to break into the reserve team and at the same time I used to train with the first team squad. Mr Robson decided to take me under his wing and he could not do enough for me. He was living at Capel St. Mary at that time and one day he mentioned that I could come and live at his house. It was a nice gesture but I told him I was settled where I was in my new digs in Ipswich.

Life in Ipswich moved quickly for me. After playing in the Football Combination when I was sixteen I was given a further

14

boost when Mr Robson included me in the first team squad that went every November for a few days break to Magaluf in Spain.

That was a month before my seventeenth birthday and it was great. To have the chance to sample life at first team level even though it would be sometime before I made my breakthrough with my debut against Manchester United at Old Trafford in August 1972 when I was still only eighteen. Before that I signed professional forms at £25 per week, plus bonuses which worked out at £10 a win and £5 for a draw. It was a lot of money to me and I was able to go out and buy my first suit.

One of my early impressions of Mr Robson was that he wanted to be one of the boys, but soon found he had to distance himself from the players to be able to do the job of manager properly. He was still trying to establish himself at the club, but an incident in 1971 stands out in my mind in particular.

I had never seen a hard side to the Gaffer, but in February 1971 that all changed. Ipswich were struggling to stay in the First Division. On a cold Tuesday night we had just been beaten 4-2 by Leeds United at Portman Road. I was on dressing room duty that night responsible, with some of the other youth team players, for sweeping them out and generally making sure everything was clean and tidy after the game. All of a sudden there was a confrontation as Bill Baxter and Tommy Carroll, who were not playing in the Leeds match, had a go at the Gaffer. A punch was thrown, but in what seemed a matter of seconds, the Gaffer and Cyril Lea had sorted them out and pinned Baxter and Carroll to the floor. Up until then I had thought of Mr Robson as a mild guy but I now knew that he could be as tough as they come. I think after that I respected him even more.

At the time I had become involved in the first team squad training, I had become the Gaffer's blue eyed boy. I was never the best of trainers and I hated Friday mornings in particular. Towards the end of the training session we used to have a heading competition to see which bloke could jump the highest and head the ball which was attached to a piece of string hanging from the wall. Nine times out of ten I would win with Trevor Whymark my only serious threat. The Gaffer used to be ecstatic about it. The rest of the players ribbed me unmercifully and I simply became known as "Bobby's Boy". At the same time

Mr Robson never allowed me to become big-headed and made sure that my feet stayed firmly on the ground and the same applied to Cyril Lea.

In many ways the Gaffer and I became good friends. True, at times he wanted to criticise me, but that was because he was trying to help me. All he wanted to do was to make me a better player while at the same time I just wanted to play football.

One weakness I had was my right foot. I use it simply to stand on. So he used to have me back in the afternoons trying to improve it. He was always there to keep a watchful eye on me. In many ways he gave me preferential treatment, no doubt about it. Had it been someone else I feel I would have been treated differently, but, remember I was his "Diamond" and he wanted to make sure that everything went smoothly as far as I was concerned. He was always a very caring person, not just with me, but with all the other players. He was always very encouraging and left no stone unturned. Examples of his nature spring instantly to mind. In his early days at the club he drove a big Austin 3000 and would sometimes give me a lift home to my digs. He would often say that if I kept working hard I would be driving around in something similar. It was not just me he would say it to, it was all the other kids as well.

The Gaffer once told me that the hardest part of his job was when he had to tell young players that he would have to let them go from the club. I can remember the day when Kenny Sharp, with whom I used to share digs, came home in tears after being told that there was no future for him at Portman Road. Although Kenny found it hard at the time Mr Robson told him that he would do all he could to fix him up with another club. He was as good as his word and Kenny joined Grimsby Town.

In the early years as a first team player there was always beer on the coach home from away trips. If we had a good win somewhere up North, the beer used to slip down that much more easily. Once we got back to Portman Road the Gaffer demanded that we gave him our car keys. He knew that we would like to go and let our hair down but there was no way he would let us drive. There was just another example of how he thought of everything and, in particular, his players.

If Mr Robson had a fault it was the case that he would

16

often repeat himself. Team talks used to drag out as he often said the same thing over and over again. One exception was when we played St. Etienne in the quarter-finals of the UEFA Cup. The first leg was in France and St. Etienne were the hot favourites as they had not lost a home tie in Europe in the previous twenty years.

All the Gaffer said before we left the dressing room was, "Don't worry what you read in the papers, nobody has given us a chance, so go out and play your normal game and don't worry about them".

That is just what we did and gave what I believe is the best performance by an Ipswich Town side in the history of the club. Mr Robson's management skills came over during the half time interval. Even though we had been well on top after gaining a goal, he had a right go at us. It was done to make sure that we wouldn't relax, and it worked a treat as we went on to win that first leg, 4-1.

During my first full season in the first team we were drawn to play St Johnstone in the Texaco Cup. We arrived in Perth in the afternoon of the day before the game so the Gaffer had us training. We had a good session and we went through some set routines, corners and freekicks. After finishing we got changed and headed for dinner and then an early night.

Next morning, before breakfast, the Gaffer said that instead of training we would have a good walk around the golf course in the hotel grounds.

While walking, having a laugh and a joke, I spotted the Gaffer, who was busy reading a paper while he walked. Oblivious to everything, he was heading straight towards a very large bunker. I told the lads but they said nothing. A few strides later and in goes the boss. The sand was flying everywhere and when he stood up he had sand in his ears, his mouth, his hair, and probably anywhere else sand can get. We all fell about simply pissing ourselves with laughter.

"Why did no-one say anything", roared Bobby Robson.

I got off the ground and said, "Well boss, you are always telling us that we have no vision, so we have seen nothing".

"I'll kill you buggers", the boss said and he walked away to get cleaned up.

For months after, we knew the boss was a keen golfer, we used to ask him how his bunker shots were getting on. In the end he saw the joke, thankfully he did not hurt himself.

The night before the biggest game of my career, the F.A. Cup Final against Arsenal, the Gaffer came up to me and said, "Beat, Jack Steggles would like to do an interview with you and I have given him the thumbs up, but it is up to you."

"No bother boss. Jack is a great bloke. He has been good to me with interviews, so I have no problem."

The Gaffer called Jack and said that it was all right and Jack said he would do it in my room. When he knocked on my door, I opened it and said, "O.K. pal, want to do it in the lobby."

"Well the boss said in your room, Beat", replied Jack.

"Piss off mate, let's go down there and see what's going on."

On our way down the corridor, the Gaffer popped his out of his room and said, "What's going on?"

I told him that Micky Lambert was asleep so we are having a chat in the lobby.

"O.K. son, but Jack, look after him."

"Don't worry Bobby, he will be o.k."

Why the Gaffer said that I don't know but it turned out right. After Jack had done the story he escorted me back to my room. On the way I stopped off to clean my shoes on one of those shoe cleaning machines they have in hotels and what the hell happened, yes The Beat got his foot stuck in the machine. Jack was going ape shit, he told me that Bobby had asked me to look after you and this happens. He was concerned that we would not get another interview. I got my foot out and told him not to worry as no-one else knows.

Well they do now, but thanks Jack, for not only being a great reporter but also a mate.

At the start of the chapter, I said how the Gaffer had taken me under his wing and made a fuss of me. I had become an important player to him and I was also a firm favourite with the supporters. Often on match days he would give me a fitness test in full view of the supporters. To be honest, I knew the day before that I would play but the Boss insisted I had one. When it was over he told me to go straight back to the dressing room and not to speak to anyone. He would tell the crowd I was playing just to gee them up.

Having played under him for so many years there is no doubt that Mr Robson was, and still is, for that fact, a brilliant manager.

3

How it all started

I was born in the George Street Maternity Home in Carlisle
on December 18th 1953. I was named Thomas Kevin Beattie and
I was the second child of nine that my parents Tommy and
Mary had. I have four other brothers and four sisters. My Dad
was a coalman and my Mum worked part time at Liptons Tea
Rooms. We did not have much, but my Mam and Dad did their
best for us.

My dad Tommy liked a drink and sometimes used to pay
mam her money and then went to the pub, the Magpie Inn at
Botcherby. He used to play darts and dominoes and when he
won, which was most of the time, we got a treat of fish and
chips on a Friday.

My old man had the chance of playing in goal for Aston
Villa, but there was more money down the mines. He was a
bugger when he had a whisky in him and I can recall the times
when I had to pull him off my mother so he would not hurt her.
I think he got the message when one night I laid him out for
picking on my mam. He never threatened her after that.

I can recall my first day at school, at St. Cuthbert's Roman
Catholic School. On the first morning I screamed the place
down. When it came to playtime I was as quiet as a mouse. Mr
Rafferty, the games teacher, gave me a ball so I could have a kick
about in the yard and from that moment Mr Rafferty was to
play a big part in my future. I was happy playing football, but I
was a nightmare in the classroom.

We had some good players in the school team, Peter Brown,
Andrews, Rafferty, David Geddis who was later to be a
colleague at Ipswich, Steve McAllindon, Murrey, Cummings,
O'Mahoney, and others for which I am sorry lads if I have
missed any of you out, but I am trying to have a get together of
all the old boys sometime in the future.

20

I started out as a goalkeeper which I loved because my dad was a goalie. Then Mr Rafferty found it hard to find a position for me, but I told him I would play anywhere. Mr Rafferty would give you his version, but I passed my 11-plus and could have gone to Grammar School, but no way, they didn't play football there, so I went to St. Patrick's School. While at St Pats, Carlisle United players used to come and try and do a bit of coaching. It was fun and they taught us quite a bit. I was in the first team and still scoring loads of goals.

Later Mr Rafferty was to write the following about myself and David Geddis.

"Way back in 1963 I first came across Kevin Beattie in the school playground at St. Cuthbert's School, Carlisle. The school was lcoated on an island site, with busy streets on three sides and a lane on the fourth, on the other side of which was a high walled bakery that did nothing to enhance the view from the classroom window.

For four days of the week the only playing space we had was a small playground, always hopelessly overcrowded at break times, and even when only one class was in the yard, trying to carry out any P.E. with forty children was problematic to say the least. Despite these drawbacks, St. Cuthbert's more often than not managed to turn out some useful sides in the years in which I was in charge of games. Once a week we had the use of a pitch in some public playing fields and although these were over half a mile away across several streets, which had to be negotiated with care, after coping with a claustrophobic yard and Victorian classrooms, getting on to wide open grass spaces was always a tonic.

Kevin soon won his place in the school team in the third year of the junior school. At first he played as a goalkeeper, a position he seemed to enjoy, and other things being equal, he might have stayed there, but it soon became evident that he would be much more effective playing out of goal.

In his fourth year in the junior school, deciding where to play Kevin in the team was something of a problem, since he was so strong both in attack and defence. I found a solution of sorts by putting four players on the halfway line with Kevin under instruction to join up with the forwards as the opportunities presented themselves. The ploy seemed to work reasonably well. Including friendlies, the school played some twenty matches that year and Kevin averaged over two goals a

21

match. We lost only one game, 3-2, regrettably the K.O. Cup Final.

I occasionally saw Kevin play at secondary school level. On one occasion I watched him playing for Cumberland boys at outside left, where I thought he was wasted. On leaving school, Kevin played for a church youth team called Blackfriars that I managed for a short time, and I was completely convinced he could make his way as a professional footballer. I tried to get Carlisle United to take an interest in him, but nothing came of it. The following year the Blackfriars team folded up from lack of numbers and Kevin joined another youth team, St. Augustine's on the north side of the city, and from there he went to Ipswich Town.

Another St. Cuthbert's pupil who was to be taken on by Ipswich Town was David Geddis. The only positions David wanted to play in were on the forward line, and indeed, it seemed he was never at ease in a defensive position. A whole hearted player, like Kevin Beattie gifted with great strength and stamina, once on the field he never stopped running.

Over the years I followed the careers of these two players with interest. Naturally I was highly pleased that while playing for Ipswich, Kevin not only gained international honours but became an outstanding member of the England team. Subsequently there was a double satisfaction for me when both Kevin and David obtained F.A. Cup winners' medals with Ipswich in 1978. Inevitably, perhaps, when watching the Final I found myself recalling the days when they played for St. Cuthbert's on Melbourne Park. I must admit that I also enjoyed a certain satisfaction that my judgement that both Kevin Beattie and David Geddis could make their mark as professional footballers had been completely vindicated."

I was picked to play for Carlisle Schoolboys when I was thirteen, but had only one game and I was never picked to play for my county schoolboys team. I don't know why, despite being recommended by various people. By the time I left St. Patrick's the school had been renamed and was taught by nuns as well as ordinary teachers. I left the school at Christmas but I was able to play in the cup final. The game was the local schools cup final so I was pleased.

The game was at Brunton Park, the home of Carlisle United and it was the first time I had played there and did not let the team down by scoring two and going on to win the cup for the first time in the school's history. We had a party back at the school and the nuns were great. What a time for Cardinal Newman School. The nuns were all dancing and jigging around and I think they had more than Coke in their glasses!

I had so many mates when I was a kid, my biggest being Steven Ullrich. We went everywhere together and in fact Steven is godfather to one of my nieces. We used to have a great time playing dykey, dykey, which is jumping over neighbours hedges. Girls were not a big thing to me but I liked a girl called Joyce a lot. I hoped she married a man who was as good looking as I am. Ha Ha!

Another mate was Podge, he was Steven's big brother. We used to have a few battles to see who was the hardest in Botcherby where we lived. I think we both came out on top. When we see each other we have a crack about those days. Rock on Podge. My two best mates at school were Steve Fontana and John Manuel, who was not at our school, but we always met after school.

Steve's mum and dad owned a fish and chip shop and Mannie's mum and dad had an ice cream business. We used to go to a place just outside Carlisle in a Robin Reliant three wheeler. We used to bomb up and down the fields for hours and sometimes not get home until 10 o'clock.

My mum and dad did not say a lot because Mr & Mrs Fontana always gave us fish and chips and guess what was for afters - yes, ice cream.

I would like to get all the guys together for a big party because it would be great to bring everybody back together again and hopefully when I am up in Carlisle signing a few books we can do this.

When I left school, I took a job as a machine fitter, but a few weeks later Liverpool asked me for a trial. Peter Thompson the ex-Liverpool player was doing some scouting around Carlisle because that was his home town. He asked me if I would like to have a trial for Liverpool. I was thrilled, but I would have to ask my dad. My dad was fine, so it was off to Liverpool. I had a week's trial and thought I did well. I was told to go home and wait for the post and I was over the moon when a few days later I got a letter.

Liverpool had asked me to play in the reserves the following Saturday in a Central League game. The Friday night before the game they asked me to go to Lime Street Station, Liverpool, where someone would meet me. I got there and for the next two hours I was talking to a porter who was Liverpool crazy and he said he had seen no one, so I decided to get the train home. A week later I got a letter from Mr Shankly to say that Liverpool had washed their hands of me as I had not turned up. I rang the club and explained the situation, but that was that. Later, when I was playing for Ipswich Town and England Bill Shankly asked me to play in his testimonial at Anfield and what a great honour I told him. The Liverpool team played an England XI and the game was superb. The crowd got what they paid for. I think the final result was something like 9-7 and after the game the great Bill Shankly handed me an envelope.

"No thanks, Mr Shankly," I said. "It was an honour for me to play in your game.

He then said "Let me tell you a secret son, I don't want it to go any further".

"O.K.", I said.

He said: "I have not made many mistakes in my time, but you were one of the biggest. Letting you go, I must have been mad".

Being told Liverpool didn't want me was a great disappointment even though it was not my fault and during the next year I could not settle. I must have had twenty jobs including one for just two hours which was in a laundry where I was a chippie. Now you might ask what a chippie does in a laundry. Well it's someone who chips the shit off the blankets and shirt tails in an old people's home. I soon left there. Even though I wasn't the best chippie in the world, the heat would have done me in.

My final job was as a van boy. I had to help the driver carry things for Dixons furniture shop and it was great. I was outdoors all the time. I was playing for St. Augustines on Saturdays and Blackfriars on Sundays. I was knocking in goals left, right, and centre. I scored eight in one game and I still think it is a record to this day. I also got my first mention in the local newspaper. My progress had obviously not gone unnoticed and one day, John Carruthers who was a northern scout for Ipswich Town watched me play, and after the game asked me to go to Ipswich for a trial .

My dad was quite happy for me to go and at that time I had never heard of Ipswich even though they were in the First Division. I was a big Carlisle and Chelsea fan. I remember the day I left for Ipswich. It was pissing down with rain and I thought what a great start. The train left heading for London Euston and I got the biggest surprise of my life when I met the chief scout for Town, Ron Gray.

In those days I was a bit shy and wasn't quite sure what to make of this huge fellow whose every other word was "marvellous". He said we were staying in a hotel for the night and we would meet the youth team at Fulham. We shared a room because he felt that I might go home in the middle of the night. I woke up in the middle of the night and nearly shit myself as there was Ron, sat in a chair with his back to the door, wearing his long johns.

"Fuck sake", I said.

Ron woke up and said, "It's only me Kevin, so go back to sleep son. Marvellous".

Next morning I played for the youth team in a South East Counties League game at Fulham. I played up front and we won. I cannot remember if I scored, but I made up for that in later games, including six at Cambridge United. Well we travelled back to Ipswich on the team coach. I was put into digs with Roger Verdi, Kenny Sharpe, Bruce Twamley, Donny Wilson and Stevie Buckle.

The landlady also had about four or five kids so a couple of the lads stayed in a caravan in the garden. The landlady had a room built just for the players but she used to stick her kids in with us and go and sit in the front room for some peace and quiet. I got really pissed off with this and told the boss because there was no privacy, so he sent me home for a fortnight and then got me new digs.

Kenny Sharpe and I moved into Redwing Close, Chantry. I still live in the area today and our landlady was Mrs Strawn, Vera she liked to be called. She was and still is brilliant and she treated us like her own. Her husband had died earlier so she had her son Steven and daughter Sue in the house. Kenny did not make the grade so left for home at the end of the season. Steve was to become my best man and we were like brothers.

We went everywhere together and he used to wind Vera up by saying, "I suppose I have sausages while the Beat has steak".

Now Vera is one lady who does not mind a swear about, so the more we wound her up, the bluer the air got. I had my first ever holiday abroad with Steve and we went to Magaluf in Majorca. What a fortnight that was and I think that is where I learned to drink because Steve liked a pint and could knock back the old Cuba Libra's.

Steve was also best man at my wedding and is a great guy. On Saturday nights we used to go to the local for a couple of pints or pop into Stone Lodge Youth Club which was just across the road from the digs. That is the place where I met Maggie and married her two years later on June 8th 1974.

4

Debut at Old Trafford

When I look back on my career, one of the highlights was undoubtedly the day I made my first debut at Old Trafford, the Theatre of Dreams, at the age of eighteen, which was quite a young age in those days, but now players of seventeen are making the big time debut in the Premiership. It was the opening match for the 1972/73 season, but I had no idea I was about to play in front of a crowd of over 51,000 until a few hours before the kick-off.

I had been picked for the squad and headed north on the Friday and thought that Bobby Robson had taken me along for a bit of experience. Robson used to take one or two of the young lads to away games to let them feel what it was like to be with the first team, staying in the best hotels, having marvellous food and being looked after like stars.

It was just after lunch at the team meeting at the Swan Inn at Bucklow Hill in the Manchester suburbs that Robson announced the side. I was amazed when he read out my name, in fact I nearly passed out. I didn't have a clue that I was going to play and my first thought was that I wanted to get in touch with my dad to let him know. I knew where he would have been, the Magpie Inn at Botcherby where we lived in Carlisle.

After the meeting I told Robson that I wanted to let my Dad know.

He said, "Don't worry son, as he is already on his way with John Carruthers".

"Great" I said, "I won't let you down boss".

"I know you won't", he said "that is why you are in the side. You have had very good pre-season and now it's time for you to shine".

Robson also explained that if he had told me I was playing on the Friday night, I might have worried and had a sleepless night which could have affected my game. He was probably right, looking back.

When the coach drove us up to the ground there was a sea of red and white outside Old Trafford. When we got to the changing rooms I settled in by getting a programme and going for a crap. I think this time, it was one of the longest I have ever had. I never liked going to look at the pitch before a game so I just started to get ready in my own mind and in my own way. I was playing as number three, left back, so I sat for a while and started to focus my mind on their right winger Willie Morgan.

After a while Cyril Lea, our coach, came up to me and told me just to show him the line because with my pace and power he would never get past. When the bell went it was time to go out. All the lads wished me all the best. When you walk up the tunnel at Old Trafford you can just see a small part of the far stand in front of you, but not hear much noise. When you get onto the pitch it's like being hit in the face with a brick, the noise was unbelievable.

The game went so fast I cannot remember a lot about it, you have to concentrate. I can remember making the pass for Trevor Whymark to score the winning goal and also that Ian Collard had marked George Best out of the game. In the dressing room after the match everybody was going mad because the press and T.V. said we had no chance.

Afterwards in the players bar Bobby Charlton came up to me and said, "Well played".

It was great to rub shoulders with the likes of Best, Charlton and Dennis Law and I felt a million dollars. I went round getting all the United players autographs and Dennis Law said to me: "You will be doing this for other players in the not too distant future".

It was a great feeling. Here I was chatting to some of the greatest stars in the game and I hoped it would last a long, long time. My dad was in his element as all the beer and food was free, so by the time he left to drive home, with John Carruthers, he was pissed. Poor old John could only have one because he was driving, but I heard he made up for it when he got back to Carlisle that night.

Three days later we played Norwich City in our first home

match and the euphoria of the United game soon disappeared. Almost 30,000 people were packed into Portman Road with the home supporters expecting us to carry on where we had left off at Old Trafford. The highs and lows of the great game of football could not be better illustrated as I was on cloud nine after winning at Manchester United but felt like shit after our East Anglian rivals had beaten us 2-1, and to cap it all, I gave away a penalty into the bargain.

I missed the next game over Birmingham City. It was a 2-0 victory, but was back in the team for Leeds United and scored my first goal in the 3-3 draw with my right foot. Yes, you are not hearing things, it was my right foot. In those days I always had my hair long and Robson used to get onto me all the time to get it cut, but my excuse was if I do boss, I would be like Samson and lose all my strength.

After the Leeds game I remember Robson asking Don Revie what he thought about my long hair.

Revie simply said: "I couldn't care less if his hair was down to his arse as long as he can play the way we know he can".

On the other side of the coin it was after that match that Robson christened me his Diamond, and for weeks afterwards the lads used to rib me unmercifully. It turned out to be a great season for both me and the club. A fourth place finish in the First Division enabled us to qualify for the UEFA Cup for the first time in the club's history, and in addition we won the Texaco Cup by beating our biggest rivals Norwich in the final. To cap off an unbelievable season, I was voted Player of the Year. It had been a long season, but I just loved playing and it didn't matter to me how many games I played, as I would rather play than train. Too many players and managers moan about the number of games they have to play in a season. What the hell are they on about? They get paid very well, so my motto was the more games the merrier.

When I looked back on my first full season it could have been a case of having to wait for my chance as the previous season I had been playing regularly for the reserves, but in the pre-season build up I was part of the first team squad.

During the summer Robson had been trying to buy Willie Maddren from Middlesbrough. When I heard that, I really got my head down as I wanted that number six shirt. The news that the boss wanted Willie acted as an incentive and as a result I had a good pre-season. In the end Maddren didn't want to move. If he had come to Ipswich I wonder if Robson would have played me at number three even though my best place was in the number six shirt. Football is about having the chance and taking it with both hands. I can look back at my first season with a great deal of satisfaction.

The 1973-1974 season was another one full of excitement although it had its share of disappointments. I didn't miss a game in any competitions as we finished fourth again in the First Division and reached the quarter-finals of the UEFA Cup. Obviously the European adventure stands out and playing the great Real Madrid in the first leg was a highlight in itself. The result was a real feather in our caps because the press had given us no chance.

Real Madrid were one of the biggest clubs in the world at the time. We played them at Portman Road and we could have won by more, but it finished 1-0 and nobody gave us much chance in the second leg. Well we certainly shut them up. The stadium was full to capacity with 80,000 mad Real supporters. The whole of our team played well. We were never put under too much pressure, but we defended so well that night that if we had played for three hours they would still not have scored and we even had a few chances. I had a header well saved and at the end of ninety minutes the score was 0-0. What a result. We were now through to the next round.

Next came Lazio with the second leg to be played in Rome and this was one of the most frightening games I have ever played in. The first leg at Portman Road went great with Trevor Whymark outstanding, and we won 4-0 and Trevor scored all four goals and it could, and perhaps should, have been more. The only bad thing that happened was that David Johnson was kicked all over the place and in the end one of their players went so over the top that he split Jonty's bollocks and he had to be carried off for stitches. I remember popping into the treatment room to see the Doc sewing him up. Not a pretty sight. I remember their centre forward Chinaglia who used to play for Cardiff so he spoke good English.

He said to me "Wait till we come to Rome. That tackle on Johnson was nothing".

In Rome both their players and supporters were so intimidating and when Colin Viljoen scored from a penalty, he ran the length of the pitch to hide behind our goalkeeper David Best. Mind you it didn't help that before the game Trevor Whymark was presented with a trophy by the Roma president for scoring all four goals at Ipswich and that was on the pitch so all the fans could see.

As Roma and Lazio both played at the Olympic Stadium in Rome and are great enemies, that didn't go down too well with the fans.

The night before the game their supporters sat outside our hotel hooting horns and letting off fireworks to try to prevent us sleeping. The Doctor had given us sleeping pills so we did not hear a thing. When the final whistle went we were chased off the field and I remember Chinaglia taking a swing at our goalkeeper, David Best. That was a bad thing to do as Bestie was a big man and the next time I saw Chinaglia his nose was bleeding and Bestie had a smile on his face.

We all got back to the changing rooms and had to put benches up against the door to keep people out. After half an hour the noise calmed down and there was a knock on the door. We opened it and in walked the doctor who was as white as a ghost. We had to wait three hours before we could leave the stadium in our coach out of the city, so we could have a quiet meal.

We came to this restaurant. It was nice and quiet and we started eating when in walked ten Lazio fans. Big Al, Bestie, Brian Simpson our physio, and myself grabbed a bottle each because they were coming our way. We stood up but the Lazio fans put out their hands to shake ours and said we were the best team they had played against for a long time. Mind you we had given them Ipswich Town Football Club ties and pennants. They were over the moon and happy men.

After beating F.C. Twente Enschede of Holland in the third round we really started to fancy ourselves to win the UEFA Cup. In the quarter-finals we went out on penalties to Locomotiv Leipzig of East Germany and it was a great shame.

We knew we could win, but luck was not with us that night. We beat the Germans 1-0 at Portman Road and they were so lucky as we hit the bar twice, the post once, and had a certain penalty turned down. Our task was made even harder when our skipper Mick Mills was sent off after twenty minutes of the second leg. The big man Allan Hunter had been absolutely magnificent all night, but was eventually to be the fall guy.

It was the big Irishman who missed the sudden-death penalty that put us out but nobody blamed him. Allan did not want to take the penalty as we had talked about that before the game, but we had a couple of young lads in that night and being the professional he was, he faced up to the pressure of taking such a crucial kick before a partisan crowd of 37,000 (well done, big man).

Our cup season was over as the previous month we had lost out to Liverpool at Anfield in the F.A. Cup fifth round. There were hopes of a long cup run especially after we had knocked out, the holders, Manchester United at Old Trafford with yours truly scoring the only goal. Although we had only the Texaco Cup to show for our efforts over the past two seasons, Ipswich Town had now established themselves as one of the leading teams in the country and in Europe as well.

There were high hopes on two cup fronts but we failed in the closing stages. In the Football League Cup, rivals Norwich City knocked us out in the fifth round replay at Ipswich and it was Johnny Miller, who had left us and signed for Norwich a month earlier, who had scored both goals.

But it was the F.A. Cup that was the real sickener as Wembley was well within our sights of what would have been Ipswich Town's first ever final appearance, but Clive Thomas the referee virtually ended those hopes in our semi-final replay against West Ham at Stamford Bridge.

In the first game at Villa Park it was a tight game. I thought we were the better side, but could not get the ball in the net. Trevor Whymark played left half and I went up front with four minutes to go. The ball came across and I got my head to it. The ball was on its way in but hit a divot which just sent it wide of the post, and I also had another effort saved by the 'keeper.

The replay, at Stamford Bridge, was a much tighter affair as both teams didn't want to give too much away. The ball came to Bryan Hamilton and he turned and scored and we were all over him when Thomas blew his whistle.

I ran up and said, "What was that for ref?"

"Offside" he said.

"Fuck off" I said, "I was forty yards away and could see he was well on. Go and check with your linesman", because the linesman had not raised his flag.

"I don't have to", he said.

"How could you say that was offside? They had two men behind him", I replied.

"Don't argue or you will go in the book".

We played on, but the game seemed to be going against us with decisions going in favour of West Ham and luck not being with us. I can even remember them having three men offside and Thomas waving play on. I also thought that when Alan Taylor scored their goal that he handled it. Thomas gave it and when you get a guy like that against you it really makes you wonder.

Clive Thomas also gave a very strange decision against Bryan Hamilton when he was playing for Everton against Liverpool in an F.A. Cup semi-final. Bryan scored a goal which was disallowed for no reason whatsoever and Thomas even admitted it in a book a year or so later. Then there was the decision in the World Cup Finals when he blew the whistle when the ball was in full flight from a corner and Brazil scored. That was an unbelievable decision which caused uproar at the time. Personally I don't think he liked Ipswich or their players and he cost us the semi-final against West Ham.

5

Called up by England

Playing for your country should be one of the greatest honours to come the way of any professional footballer. So when Don Revie picked me for the European Championship qualifying match against Cyprus at Wembley in April, 1975, I could not have been more delighted.

Considering the problem I had had a year earlier when I failed to turn up for an England Under-23 match and put my international career in jeopardy, it was a proud moment when I walked out at Wembley for what I had hoped would be the first of many caps.

In the end I managed only nine games, including two as a substitute. I had been selected on countless occasions, but had to withdraw because of the problems with my knee. It is something that will haunt me for the rest of my life.

Had I been able to keep fit, I reckon I would have played over 100 times for my country and joined an elite group of players that have achieved that landmark.

One thing I can claim, however, is that I was a World Cup winner. I played in the England team that won the Little World Cup when we beat West Germany in the final in Barcelona. I remember playing at the back with Liverpool's Phil Thompson in the 2-1 victory and after the match we were each presented with a watch.

After tasting success at international level, I wanted more of it. The next step up the ladder was the Under-23s, but it could have been the end for me after I decided not to play in Scotland.

It was an impromptu decision on my part, but one that was to make the headlines. I had caught the train from Ipswich to travel to Scotland via London. When the train from Euston to Glasgow pulled in at Carlisle I decided to get off and go and see my family.

To be honest I was tired and didn't feel like playing. Our first daughter Emma had recently been born and I wasn't sleeping too well. I felt I had made the right decision at that time, but was obviously unawares of the consequences.

Bobby Robson rang me the next day and told me to get back to Ipswich.

Imagine my surprise, however, when I was called up for the next England Under 23 game against Wales in Swansea. I thought by blotting my copybook my chances of playing for an England team again might have ended, but Don Revie was brilliant. The night before the Wales games he had a long talk with me, telling me he understood why I had bailed out. He also told me that I would soon be in the full England team if I kept up my form and he was confident that I wouldn't do anything silly again. The chat with Revie really perked me up and it was far different from the reception I had received from Robson on my return from Carlisle to Ipswich. Mind you, I had expected that.

Simply, Revie made me feel brilliant and the next night I helped repay the faith he had in me by scoring one of the England goals in a 2-0 win. The other one was scored by Trevor Whymark, so I reckoned the scoreline read Wales 0, Ipswich Town 2!

A couple of months after the Wales game, I was called into the full England squad. In those days Revie was in charge of both teams. I remember the promise he had made to me about playing for England, but I was surprised it had come so quickly after our chat.

My first game against Cyprus will always be remembered for the fact that Malcolm MacDonald scored all the goals in a 5-0 victory. In fact, it should have been remembered for Kevin Beattie scoring on his debut, but more of that later.

Although my international career was brief, there's no doubt about the highlight. I will always have a vivid memory of May 24th, 1975 when I was a member of the team that thrashed Scotland 5-1 at Wembley with me scoring one of the goals.

Three of my appearances were made at Wembley, but the last match against Holland is one I would like to forget. The Dutch ran rings round us that night in February, 1977 and I had a real stinker. I would go as far as to say it was my worst performance of my whole career and after the game I cried my eyes out. Johnny Rep, the flying Dutch winger, had given me a real roasting and I couldn't wait to get off the pitch.

One disappointing aspect of all the games I played for England was that not one was playing in my proper position in central defence. They were all at left-back.

There were plenty of disappointments to follow which in many ways were made worse by the build-up I had had in certain quarters.

Some people had already started to compare me with Manchester United's legendary defender Duncan Edwards, who died in hospital following the Munich Air Disaster.

I never saw Duncan play, but had been told what a great player he was and that I was the person who could emulate him. To be honest I never compared myself with anyone else, but I must say I got a boost when Bobby Charlton told me after an Ipswich game at Old Trafford how much I reminded him of Duncan. That was a great accolade coming from someone like Bobby.

The record books say that my last appearance in an England shirt came on October 12, 1977 when I was a substitute in the World Cup qualifier against Luxembourg. Ron Greenwood, the manager, sent me on midway through the second-half to make sure there was no scares after we had established a 2-0 lead.

Portman Road was full of international players at the time I was involved. There was always a buzz in the dressing room on a Friday morning prior to an England match which was to be played the following Wednesday. Players picked for the England squad would be notified by post and at Ipswich the letters, with the envelope bearing the England crest, would be put in the dressing room.

From my point of view, it so often became a case of being picked one day and withdrawing the next.

My knee used to blow up after our Saturday match and Bobby Robson was on the phone to the Football Association to tell them that I had to pull out. Subsequently I joined a few squads which were great fun, but it was never quite the same knowing that I wasn't going to play. Looking back, I would rather have stayed at home.

There is only one thing better than playing for you country, and that is playing and scoring. I thought I had done just that in my very first international game against Cyprus in a European Championship qualifier at Wembley on April 16th 1975.

The game will be largely remembered for the fact that Malcolm Macdonald scored all five goals in a 5-0 victory.

The truth is that I "scored" what should have been England's first goal, but it was disallowed for a foul on the goalkeeper. What happened was that we had won a corner, and being a good header of the ball, took up my position in the Cypriot penalty area. The corner came over, their goalkeeper came but failed to get it and the ball fell at my feet. It bounced up, the 'keeper made a grab for it, but I was quicker and hit the ball into the net with my knee.

At the same time the 'keeper made contact with my knee and was knocked out. I put up my hands in celebration and the crowd roared, but within seconds my jubilation had been cut short when the referee disallowed it. I was not very happy to say the least and told the referee what I thought of his decision.

The Cypriot goalkeeper was carried off and replaced by the reserve. What I will say is that if the first choice 'keeper had not been injured, Supermac would not have got five.

So he's got me to thank for establishing what was then a goalscoring record. It was later equalled by David Platt against San Marino in a World Cup qualifying match, but he missed the chance to score a sixth when he failed with a penalty.

However, the game that meant more to me than any of the others was the England-Scotland Home International at Wembley on May 24th, 1975. It was a fixture that meant more to the Scottish supporters and they were definitely in the majority amongst a full house.

It was the perfect occasion for me to score one of my best ever goals during my career. We were leading 1-0 at the time when Scotland earned a corner at the tunnel end of the ground. The ball came over, but I managed to get my head to it and knock it out to Alan Ball.

"Bally" held the ball up and waited for someone to make a break from defence and he soon found that Kevin Keegan had made a great run down the right. At the same time I noticed that nobody was up front, so I decided to make a long run through the middle.

Alan played the ball to Keegan while I just kept on running. KK delivered the perfect cross, I had timed my run to perfection, and the end result was that I headed the ball into the far top corner of the net.

The Scotland goalkeeper collided with the post in an attempt to save my header, but he had no chance. Then the celebrations started. I ran over to Kevin to tell him what a terrific cross he had put in and he congratulated me on a smashing goal.

Then all the lads swarmed over me while the crowd were going bananas. It was one of the greatest feelings of my life and we went on to slaughter the Scots 5-1 with the other goalscorers being Gerry Francis (2), Colin Bell and, my then team-mate, David Johnson, completing the rout.

What a weekend that was and I received so many letters congratulating me on my goal. They must have taken a month to read.

When I watch England play now and somebody scores I still get that tingling feeling despite the fact that my Wembley goal was more than twenty years ago.

I always want England to do well and am proud that I have represented my country, although, of course, it should have been many more times.

INTERNATIONAL CAPS

APRIL 16, 1975 v Cyprus (European Championship qualifier) at Wembley.
Won 5-0.
Shilton. Madeley, Watson, Todd, BEATTIE, Bell, Ball, Hudson, Channon, Macdonald, Keegan. Sub: Thomas.
Scorers: MacDonald (5).

MAY 11, 1975 v Cyprus (European Championship) in Limassol.
Won 1-0.
Clemence, Whitworth, BEATTIE, Watson, Todd, Bell, Thomas, Ball, Channon, MacDonald, Keegan. Subs: Hughes and Tueart.
Scorer: Keegan.

MAY 24, 1975 v Scotland (Home International) at Wembley.
Won 5-1.
Clemence, Whitworth, BEATTIE, Bell, Watson, Todd, Ball, Channon, Johnson, G.Francis, Keegan. Sub: Thomas.
Scorers: G.Francis (2), Bell, Beattie, Johnson.

SEPTEMBER 3, 1975 v Switzerland (European Championship qualifier) in Basle.
Won 2-1.
Clemence, Whitworth, Todd, Watson, BEATTIE, Bell, Currie, G.Francis, Channon, Johnson, Keegan. Sub: MacDonald.
Scorers: Keegan, Channon.

NOVEMBER 19, 1975 v Portugal (European Championship qualifier) in Lisbon.
Drew 1-1.
Clemence, Whitworth, BEATTIE, G.Francis, Watson, Todd, Keegan, Channon, MacDonald, Brooking, Madeley. Subs: Thomas and Clarke.
Scorer: Channon

OCTOBER 13, 1976 v Finland (World Cup qualifier) at Wembley.
Won 2-1.
Clemence, Todd, BEATTIE, Thompson, Greenhoff, Wilkins, Keegan, Channon, Royle, Brooking, Tueart. Subs: Mills, Hill.
Scorers: Royle, Tueart.

NOVEMBER 17, 1976 v Italy (World Cup qualifier) in Rome.
Lost 2-0.
Clemence, Clement, Mills, Greenhoff, McFarland, Hughes, Keegan, Channon, Bowles, Cherry, Brooking. Sub: BEATTIE.

FEBRUARY 9, 1977 v Holland (Friendly) at Wembley.
Lost 2-0.
Clemence, Clement, BEATTIE, Doyle, Watson, Madeley, Keegan, Greenhoff, T. Francis, Bowles, Brooking. Subs: Pearson, Todd.

OCTOBER 12, 1977 v Luxembourg (World Cup qualifier) in Luxembourg.
Won 2-0.
Clemence, Cherry, Watson, Hughes, Kennedy, Callaghan, McDermott, Wilkins, T Francis, Mariner, Hill. Subs: BEATTIE, Whymark.
Scorers: Kennedy, Mariner.

6

Badly Burned

Easter Sunday, 1977, is a date that sticks in the memory, but for all the wrong reasons. The previous day we had beaten old rivals Norwich City 1-0 at Carrow Road with a goal from Trevor Whymark and were looking forward to sustaining our challenge for the First Division title when Birmingham City were visitors to Portman Road on Easter Monday afternoon.

A restful Sunday had been the plan. I had a lay-in and then decided to do a spot of gardening. My father-in-law had given me an old oil drum so that I could burn all the rubbish. After I had lit it I went indoors for something and when I returned I thought the fire had gone out. To get it going again I decided to use some petrol

What I didn't know was that the fire was still alight and when I emptied the can of petrol flames leapt up from the oil drum. In a moment of panic I threw the can down, but the petrol splattered all over me.

I rushed indoors and grabbed a towel to rub myself down because my shirt had caught alight. Then I wrapped the towel around my neck. I called Maggie who was pregnant at the time with our second daughter Sarah. Maggie went across the road immediately to ask our neighbour, Bob Aldred, if he could take me to the hospital. Bob didn't have a car, so he used mine and in the rush to get me to hospital, he drove into my front wall and put a dent in the car!

What a nightmare!

It was not until I reached the hospital that I realised I had been badly burned. The petrol had caught my face, hair, a little of my body, but worst of all my neck. The hospital staff took one look at me and decided I would be staying in for a while. I was put in isolation and on a drip, but the funny thing was that I couldn't feel a thing apart from a nasty stinging feeling on my nipples. The first chance I had to look in a mirror was not a pretty sight. Skin was hanging off me and any visitors had to wear masks which I found amusing considering I had opened the windows and was sitting in bed smoking!

Altogether I was to spend the next eight weeks in hospital. What I didn't realise at the time was that my nerve ends had been burned, and after a fortnight I was in agony. It was the worst pain I have had in my life and even today when I see people on television that have been burned, it makes me shudder. I was put into a private ward next door to a woman who had been badly burned by oil from a chip pan. She was worse off than me, but what had intended to be a relaxing day in the garden had turned into a nightmare.

What was worse was the fact while I was laying in hospital, the newspapers rounded on Maggie. On the second night one national tabloid had got hold of the story that Maggie had thrown a chip pan of burning oil all over me. Maggie told them that it was completely untrue, but they wouldn't accept it.

They persisted in setting up camp on our doorstep and pestered Maggie until she couldn't take any more. As we were not on the phone at the time, that made things more difficult for Maggie. The newspaper people decided to shine their headlights into our front window. That was the final straw as far as Maggie was concerned. She persuaded her father to go to the phone box up the road and ring the police who told them to clear off.

That wasn't the end of it. Next day the same people from the newspaper came back and started questioning my neighbours, and even my doctor. For days Maggie was virtually a prisoner in her own home.

To this day, almost 20 years on, some people still believe Maggie threw a chip pan of oil over me. Had she done so, I would have been scarred for life. The bonfire accident obviously put an end to me playing for the rest of the 1976-77 season. Although we beat Birmingham the following day, three successive defeats followed, including the crunch match against fellow title chasers Liverpool.

In fact we won only one of the final seven games the team had to play without me and finished third behind winners

Liverpool and Manchester City.

Bobby Robson had been desperate to win the Championship and that season had given him one of his best chances. The fact that I wasn't able to play in those last seven games was a big blow to him, and while I was laying in my hospital bed powerless to do anything. I knew deep down that had I been able to play we would have had a great chance of fulfiling the manager's dream.

7

My Lucky Escape

My hopes of playing in an F.A. Cup Final could have disappeared just ten days before the big day at Wembley.

No, it was not my knee that was the problem this time - although, of course, I wasn't 100 per cent fit - but a car crash that could have easily written off myself, Robin Turner and my mate Barry Nunn.

The three of us had popped up the Gainsborough Labour Club in the afternoon and that evening went down the First Floor Club for a few drinks. Robin had an old Triumph 2000 at the time and when we left the First Floor he was going to drive us home, but we had only gone barely a quarter of a mile when we crashed into a lamp post in Fore Street.

I was sitting in the back of the car and for a laugh decided to take off my knee bandage and put it over my face. The next moment there was a big bang and we had hit a lamp post outside Fore Street swimming pool.

The lamp post was demolished, the car a write-off and it was a miracle that none of us was severely injured. In fact, we got away with hardly a scratch.

It is not an exaggeration to say that we could have been killed. Fortunately a friend of ours, Bob Shelley, had heard the bang from the taxi office further up Fore Street and came to our rescue. First we pushed the car onto the car park next to the swimming pool before Bob gave us all a lift home.

Soon afterwards I rang up Robin to say that we should agree on a story should we be confronted by Bobby Robson. We felt that he would soon get to hear about the incident - after all the police would soon find out that the car belonged to Robin - and with the F.A. Cup Final so close we did not want to land in hot water.

After training the next day we were called to his office.

Robin and I agreed that we should say a cat ran out in to the road, he swerved to avoid it and then crashed into the lamp post.

Robin went in first and when I went in I told the "gaffer" the story we had agreed upon, but Robin had forgotten the story and had told Robson that it was a dog that he tried to avoid! So when the manager told me that, I changed track and said that I was probably mistaken and that it was a small dog, something like a Jack Russell!

I was expecting a right rollicking, but in fact Robson just burst out laughing and that broke the ice. He told me he had thought of fining us a week's wages, but in the end decided against it.

It was also decided to keep quiet about the incident. With the F.A. Cup final so close, Robson didn't want anything to distract the club on their big day.

There's no doubt that the three of us — and Robin and me in particular — had had a lucky escape. There's also no doubt that without Bob Shelley who came to the rescue quickly we could have been locked up for the night besides avoiding serious injury.

The incident was forgotten as we concentrated on the final and on the Wednesday before the match we left Ipswich and went down to Hertfordshire to finalise our preparations. Robson had already decided that I would be playing. In fact, at that time my knee felt better than it had for a long time, but that was because I had not been playing.

I had played little football in the previous few months. I played in the fourth round tie against Hartlepool at Portman Road following a couple of reserve games, but we won comfortably 4-1 and I had little to do.

Robson wanted me to play in the fifth round tie at Bristol Rovers, but once he had seen the snow and icy conditions, decided not to risk me.

I was not fit enough to play at Millwall in the sixth round, but came back for the semi-final against West Bromwich Albion at Highbury.

I had a couple of jabs before the game to ease the pain, but it turned out to be one of the hardest games I had ever played in simply because I was so short of match practice. With a month between the semi-final and final, I decided that I must try and get fit and did a bit more training.

Eight days before the final Robson and I had a chat and we both agreed that I would be fit to play. What concerned him more was that I might get injured at home or doing something silly!

I was certainly fit enough although it was not until the day before the match that I decided I would definitely play. I wanted to be honest with myself and the rest of the team. Had I felt my knee wasn't up to it, I would not have played.

When we arrived at our hotel in Hertfordshire I found I was rooming with Micky Lambert, who was in his testimonial year and was substitute at Wembley. For years I had shared a room with Allan Hunter, but because I had not played for some time the big man had teamed up with skipper Mick Mills.

We were treated like gods at the hotel, but I have certainly never known a man like "Lamby" to eat as much as he did.

On the Thursday night Ted Croker, then the secretary of the Football Association, came to the hotel to talk to us about procedure in front of royalty. Princess Alexander was the guest of honour for the final and Mr Croker had already been warned about my strong handshake!

I was told to take it easy when I shook hands with her when she was presented to the teams.

On the morning of the match, we were interviewed by BBC television commentator John Motson, who talked in turn to all the players. Somebody had tipped off "Motty" that Clive Woods had a tattoo on his arm. Clive was embarrassed about the tattoo, but when he was asked about it he was proud to show it to the watching nation.

I had played for England at Wembley, but it was different playing for your club. When we first came out on the pitch about an hour before the start and saw all our supporters, we got a tingle and I knew from that moment we weren't going to lose.

When we were waiting in the tunnel waiting for the signal when both teams walked onto the pitch, I noticed that the Arsenal players looked worried, while we were so relaxed. As the players were being introduced to Princess Alexander, Paul Cooper and I were looking around the crowd trying to spot the celebrities.

We picked out Justin Hayward of the Moody Blues and Rod Stewart before the moment came when I was introduced to the Princess. On TV that morning I had said that I been told by Ted Croker to be gentle with my handshake and the Princess told me she had been watching.

We had quite a chat and that relaxed me tremendously. I was now really ready for the game.

8

Making a killing

Reaching the F.A. Cup Final was a tremendous achievement in itself, but I never dreamt how much it was going to be worth in terms of hard cash. What I'll tell you now is that most of the players at Portman Road made more out of selling cup final tickets than they received in wages and bonuses for playing and winning at Wembley from the club.

All the first team squad players were given 120 tickets and soon after I was approached by a man and asked how many tickets I could get hold of. It soon became clear that the man worked for Stan Flashman, the well known London ticket tout. A couple of days later I had a telephone call from Stan. I had never met or spoken to him in my life before and wasn't likely to meet him over this matter as he was going to send down one of his representatives to see me.

Even after I had looked after family and friends with tickets I still had 80 left, now it was time to make a killing. Most of the other players gave me their tickets and one of Stan's men came down from London to collect the tickets and a deal had been struck. Even youth team players gave me two or three tickets they had so they could also make a fast buck.

A week before the final I got a telephone call from Stan's office to say there was someone on his way down from London with the money. I was told to be at home at a certain time and as if on cue this big motor drove up and out got three huge men. One was carrying a case and the other two were minders.

I found it all very nerve-wracking. I was expecting about £20,000 but imagine my surprise when the bloke counted out £36,000 in notes.

I even got a grand as a bonus for actually doing the deal.

After Stan's men left I counted the cash again and then shit myself. What if someone saw the men coming in with the cash?

I was thinking all the bad things that could happen to me. Maggie and I were due to go out that evening so we were thinking what the hell to do with the money. Do we take it with us or hide it somewhere? I put it into a bag and hid it in the loft and we went out to dinner but were back early because of the cash. I counted it out again and put it in envelopes ready for the boys. I had made arrangements to meet the boys at the groundsman's hut two at a time at five minute intervals the following day. I'll tell you there were a lot of happy faces that day, especially the young boys who had never had so much money in their lives. Most of them brought new clothes and I remember Bobby Robson saying he must be paying them too much. If only he knew.

I had to laugh when we walked out onto the pitch before the game. When you watch the final on the television you can always see the players looking up to the stands to see their families. Well I was no exception and when I looked into the stands to see Maggie and my family, all I could see around them were people of all different nationalities under the sun.

It was a few years later that I actually met Stan in the flesh. I had just finished playing at Middlesbrough and was wondering what to do when I got a call from my old team mate Brian Talbot or Noddy as he was known as at Portman Road.

Noddy knew that Stan was a keen Arsenal fan when he played there. He was also Chairman of Barnet and asked if I could meet him at his offices near Kings Cross Railway Station. I will never forget the day of our meeting. There were bodyguards everywhere. I knew the F.A. regarded Stan as a villain, but I found him to be a nice bloke and I would never cross him.

I signed for Barnet but only stayed for six months. They were in the G.M. Vauxhall Conference but I only played two games because of my knee. Barry Fry was manager and I got on great with him. Some of the players really didn't pull their weight so I thought I would get out.

Barry is a real great guy. I have been to Peterborough recently with a couple of players and Barry has really looked after me and made me welcome. The set-up of Posh is pretty good and they have one of the best training grounds I have ever seen. I can honestly say a few Premiership clubs would envy the facilities. I would like to personally thank Barry, Chris Turner and Phil Neal for making me so welcome and if I ever got a chance to get back into football, that would be the place I would like to go.

Good luck Posh, and if you need a good defensive coach then I am your man .

9

Wembley

It had seemed a long wait, but now the final was under way. We felt there was no pressure on us because Arsenal were the firm favourites. In fact we were quoted at 5-2, an extremely generous price considering there were only two contestants and most of our players had had a few quid on us to win. Even the "gaffer" had had a bet, so confident he was on us winning.

I got my first touch early on. I took the ball off Frank Stapleton, the Arsenal striker. and made ground. Despite the 100,000 crowd and all the noise, I clearly heard our coach Cyril Lea shouting from the bench 'keep going Beat'. As far as I can recall, it was the first time I had heard what Cyril said during a match.

To be honest I can't really remember much about the first half after that. The time seemed to go so quickly. The half time interval is also a blur. The second half also seemed to fly by. I can remember John Wark hitting the post twice and that we were never under any real pressure.

As far as Roger Osborne's goal is concerned, all I remember is the ball hitting the back of the net, the arms going up before the noise really hit me. Roger looked as white as a sheet after he had surfaced from all the congratulations and soon afterwards he went off to be replaced by Mick Lambert.

The last 13 minutes seemed as long as the whole of the first half, but then the final whistle went and the celebrations really began. All I could think of was going up the steps to collect my winner's medal. I remember what seemed a long walk up the steps to the Royal Box and that somebody put a hat on my head and a scarf round my neck. When Mick Mills held the cup aloft, I have never heard a roar like it. When we got down to the bottom of the steps the other side of the Royal Box, I waited for Allan Hunter before we went on our lap of honour.

"Big Al" had managed to get hold of a couple of cigarettes and we ran round Wembley having a quick drag and hiding the cigarette in the palm of our hands! We went first to the end where the Arsenal supporters were and they applauded us. It was known as the friendly final and they knew that we had been the best side on the day and deserved to win.

When we got to the Ipswich end the reception we got from our supporters was tremendous. I have never heard anything like it. We didn't want to go to the dressing rooms, preferring to go on another lap of the stadium, but a steward wouldn't let us.

By the time we reached our dressing room the champagne had been uncorked. We jumped into the bath and drank champagne out of the F.A. Cup, something I'll never forget for the rest of my life. Most of the lads were getting dressed leaving Allan and I sitting in the bath having a cigarette and talking about the match. We both agreed it was one of the easiest games that we had played in. We had worked so well as a team and there was no way we would have been beaten.

Arsenal, we felt, would never have scored, and from my point of view I knew that I had that something extra in me.

Before the game I had had two pain-killing injections and apparently another one at half-time, but I can't remember it. It wasn't long before my knee blew up again, like a balloon, but it was something I had become used to over the past couple of years.

We left Wembley by coach to drive to the Royal Garden Hotel in Kensington for the celebrations. Cyril Lea was so proud that he sat in the front showing off the F.A. Cup to all and sundry. When we arrived at the hotel there were a great number of people waiting to greet us.

After a meeting with Bobby Robson, I bumped into Brian Cant, who introduced Play School on TV and he invited me to have a drink with him after the banquet. When we got to our rooms there was champagne from chairman Mr John Cobbold. While Maggie got ready, I decided to sit in the bath and drink more champagne. I had bought a new suit for the occasion, it was green, and in Allan Hunter's honour.

Downstairs in the hotel Mr John was buying more drinks and after the banquet Allan, Robin Turner, myself and our wives met up with Brian Cant. We decided to go out and found a nice little bar with Brian sitting there wearing my number six shirt!

Back at the hotel our wives went to bed while the rest of us carried on drinking. Suddenly I looked at my watch to see that it was 4.40 a.m. Sunday morning. I decided that I would just give Maggie a ring to see how she was and off I went to the reception to dial the number. I phoned what I thought was our room and a bloke answered the phone saying what did I think I was doing ringing him at that time . I thought there was a stranger in our room, so I raced upstairs intending to sort him out. When I got there I realised I had dialled the wrong number and when I came downstairs again the manager of the hotel was waiting for me, saying he had had a complaint from one of his guests. I apologised, saying I was drunk, but was then told the guest would like to have a word with me.

I decided it was best to sort it out, but was in trepidation when I knocked on his door. As it turned out he was an Arabian Prince and he could not have been more charming.

He told me he had flown over from Dubai to watch the final. He asked me if I would autograph some pictures and then offered me a drink. It seemed so funny because my initial reaction when he first answered the phone, that I was going to kill him!

By now it was 7.20 a.m, and I had not had a wink of sleep. I went back to my room to have a shower before breakfast was brought in. I banged my bad knee against the bed before tucking into a full English breakfast with champagne. I had just finished my breakfast when I got a call from Paul Cooper telling me to get down to the bar where he had a pint waiting for me.

It was only 9 a.m. Steve Curry from the Daily Express was also there and he ordered me a drink which he said would really settle me down. To this day I don't know what was in it, but it did the trick!

By mid-morning we were ready to head off home. The celebrations had not ended, that's for sure, but that's another story.

10

The Homecoming

Nothing went according to plan on the Sunday morning after the final. We were all supposed to leave the Royal Garden Hotel in Kensington at 9 a.m, but by the time we finally got away it was nearer 11 a.m. What really sticks out in my mind was that Cyril Lea sat drinking at the back of the bus with the boys which was something that he had never done before.

It was decided that we would stop off at the Army and Navy Pub in Chelmsford. We often stopped at this pub in the past on our way home from games in London or the South East. Anyway it was a chance to show the fans the cup.

Bobby Robson said that we could stop for half an hour to have a drink and speak to the fans, but three pints later and an hour had gone and we were still there. The people in the pub were superb, some of the men were even crying with joy. Before we left the pub I bought three bottles of wine, one for Big Al, one for Robin Turner, and the other for me.

Big Al said to me, "Give them away, I have something for you and me".

"O.K." I said.

I gave mine and Big Al's away and then the big man got out two bottles of vodka, a bottle of lemonade and two glasses.

Just as the coach was pulling out the of the car park, Al shouted,

"Stop the bus, I have forgotten something."

Robson thought he had left his medal behind, but he came back with a bag of ice.

"You can't have vodka and lemonade without ice," he said to me.

Well we fell about laughing, as you can appreciate.

As we were travelling down the A12 towards Ipswich it was brilliant. The scene is something I'll never forget. All the bridges were decorated in blue and white and there were people on the pavements waving and shouting to us. Cars were driving past with blue and white scarves hanging out of the windows. Everybody seemed so happy I felt so proud.

When we eventually arrived at Portman Road, we had to go straight on to an open topped bus for a tour through the town. There were hundreds of people around the town. The tour was meant to take three-quarters of an hour, but it took us two hours to get to the Town Hall to the reception.

When we finally got there, outside on the Cornhill which is the main centre of the town in Ipswich, was choc-a-bloc full of people. There were people literally hanging off lampposts and bus stops and anything else that they could find so as they could get a good view of the players and see the cup.

We had to go through a side door to get to the balcony but before that there was a champagne reception and then a little gap, as if we hadn't had enough to drink by then. However, as one does, you have to oblige and have one or two or three. What everybody really wanted was to get on the balcony and see the fans. One by one each player was introduced to the fans. Big Al and I were introduced as Bacon and Eggs and the noise was phenomenal. It was a hell of an experience. There was no doubt that that Sunday in 1978 was one of the proudest days of my life and it meant so much to the people of Ipswich and Suffolk that we had won the F.A. Cup for them. My mam and dad were staying at the Golden Lion Hotel which is literally a stone throw away from the Town Hall. Allan Hunter and I decided to go and see them. Our short route took us past the band that were playing in the teams honour and we had a laugh with them as well as trying to play some of the instruments before reaching the hotel.

When we got to my parents room it was full of people and overlooked the Cornhill. So big Al and I poured champagne over everybody down below us. My Dad was well pissed (well when wasn't he?), my mam was crying with joy and they had invited all the Hotel people into their room for a drink and didn't I know it when I paid the bill later on.

By the time we had finished at the Town Hall it was time for me and Robin Turner to go up to the Gainsborough Labour

Club as they had laid on party for us and what a great night we had with the G.L.C. members. All our friends were there, which are too many to mention, and I can't remember what time I got to bed. I did sleep well, and I am not surprised.

I woke up at lunch time on Monday, had something to drink and eat, and went to the ground in the afternoon, I hadn't been there very long when Allan and myself were called into Robson's office.

There we found the police waiting for us, but I hadn't a clue why. They told us that two of the trumpets that the band were using had gone missing and someone had told the police that as they had seen us messing about with some of their instruments, they were obliged to investigate the incident. We gave our explanation and that was accepted.

The police said they knew we had not taken the trumpets, but it was a good chance to get our autographs and shake our hands for winning the cup for Ipswich Town.

I remember the band were egging Allan and I to have a go on the trumpets and to this day I have always wondered what actually happened to them. Just thinking about it now, had our explanation not been accepted, we could have been locked up after one of the greatest days of our lives.

On the Monday evening we had Micky Lambert's Testimonial and the crowd were fantastic. As far as I am concerned, the Ipswich people have always been fantastic. We paraded the Cup around the ground that night and what a feeling it was.

There was one final game to go before the end of the season, which was also played during that week. A few of the lads did not play, like myself, Allan Hunter and Paul Mariner, but the points were not important as we had enough to stay up, but I do think sometimes that we could have won the Cup and possibly gone down in the same season.

When I look back at Middlesbrough's 1996-97 season, and see what happened to them, I realised now how lucky I was as a player to play in an F.A. Cup Final and win.

After the Cup Final and all the events and celebrations had finished the lads went off to Hawaii for their end of season tour. I had to go into hospital for another operation to clear out my knee. When I came out of hospital a week or so later I was asked by the gaffer if I would like to go and help Charlie Woods, the Youth team manager, on the trip to Lloret Del Mar in Spain. At the same time as helping the kids out in this prestigious tournament, it would also be bice for a bit of a holiday.

"Absolutely bloody great", I said to the Boss, "when do we leave."

When we arrived in Spain it was a nightmare because of the flying and as you may know I hate it, but we finally got settled into this little hotel right next to the beach. The hotel was not up to much but I was just very happy to be away after the season. The next morning Charlie and myself took the kids training. The pitch was rock hard so we told the boys to take things easy. We didn't want any injuries or problems before the tournament started. We had a match that evening and we won it.

Charlie told the boys that they could go out and have a couple of beers but not to get pissed. There was a twelve o'clock deadline for the boys to get in. Charlie and I sat in the lobby waiting for the boys. They came back in dribs and drabs and you could tell they had drunk more than they should have. I got them all to bed and told Charlie I was going out for a couple of pints myself with a mate of mine who lived in Spain.

The guy's name was "Big" Dave, but we nicknamed him "Shitter" because he farted all the time. I reckon it was all the food he had eaten whilst in Spain. All those paellas and olive oil had obviously caused a problem to his system. He even had a tee shirt named for him with "Shitter" plastered on the back and front and Dave wore it every day. He was over the moon with it.

Anyway, we went to a club for a drink and to our surprise there were still a couple of the boys sitting in there. They were Terry Butcher and Russell Osman.

"How the hell did you get here?", I said.

"We shimmied down the drainpipe from the hotel room", was the reply.

"O.K.", I said, "but when you get back don't make a noise. I don't want Charlie finding out."

Mind you, Terry and Russell were both on the fringe of first team football, so really I should have been setting an example to them. After a few drinks, I did say we had better get back as we had to train that afternoon.

We got back to the hotel and the more you try to be quiet the harder it becomes and in the end I fell over a big plant in the lobby. The hotel floor was marble so the noise echoed all round the hotel. We all scarpered our separate ways and tried to get up to our rooms without seeing anyone.

Unfortunately, as I was creeping to my room, the owner of the hotel came out of his room and asked what all the noise was.

"Sorry," I said, "but something ran across the hallway and made me jump and I fell over the plant."

"You're drunk," said the guy.

"Don't be silly," I replied.

He was up for reporting me to Charlie but I told him that the thing that ran across the floor was a rat, and if he reported me then I would have to tell Charlie about the hygiene in the hotel and that we would have to move out and find somewhere else for the boys to stay, and the club would then sue them for damages and expenses.

"O.K.," he said, "let's go to the bar and have a nightcap and sort things out."

Anyway after the rat story we ended up shaking hands and nothing was said for the rest of the trip. I didn't have to pay for a drink in the hotel for the remainder of our stay.

The boys did really well and got to the final of the tournament but then lost by the odd goal. The rest of the break was great, and the memories superb and I would like to thank the hotel owner for the free drinks that week. I might give him a bell and tell him I'm coming over for a couple of weeks and wonder what he would say.

11

Pre-season training

Whilst most people are thinking about holidays and hopefully days of hot sunshine, for professional footballers it is a time to knuckle down to very hard work.

Pre-season training may be a necessity to trim off the excess pounds and get in shape for the forthcoming campaign but it was not a time I personally enjoyed. We might have had a summer of rain and bad weather but I can guarantee you that when pre-season starts the sun comes out and it becomes very hot.

During Bobby Robson's reign at Portman Road we used to be put through our paces at a Naval Establishment ten miles outside Ipswich called H.M.S. Ganges in the village of Shotley. The facilities were first class and included an Olympic size swimming pool and running track, three gyms, four football pitches and we had a bit of free time in the bowling alley.

Each day we used to travel there in convoys from Portman Road in our own cars.It was the start of the '74/'75 campaign, and I remember one day in particular, when a prank that could have cost some of us our lives. At that time I was driving an Opel Manta SR. It was a very powerful car and I was giving a lift to John Wark, Robin Turner, Glen Westley, and a youth team player.

The road to Shotley is full of twists and turns and I suddenly spotted in my rear view mirror "Noddy" Talbot coming up fast behind me in his Ford Capri. "Noddy", as Brian Talbot was known at the club, overtook me and I got a ribbing from the lads saying, "you're not going to let him beat you like that". No chance, I thought, and I put my foot down. I took my opportunity on a short straight but a bend came up too quickly from my point of view.

Just as I had negotiated the bend the back of my car started to slide. I tried to correct it, but it spun round and rolled over three times and ended up upside down facing the same way from which I had just come. We all climbed out of the back window, our only escape route because the roof was jammed flat against the steering wheel. We were shaking like jelly, but miraculously the only injury was a small cut under Glen Westley's eye.

Noddy had seen everything and thought that none of us would walk away from the crash. We certainly had a very lucky escape. A few moments later the coaching staff pulled up. Charlie Woods, then the youth team coach, directed the traffic past the scene of the accident before Bobby Ferguson, who was then the reserve team coach, bundled us into his car to take us to see the doctor at H.M.S. Ganges.

In an effort to get us there as quickly as possible Fergie drove so fast that we were shitting ourselves and we were pleased when we reached our destination as at times going with Fergie in the car was worse than the actual crash.

While we were in the doctor's office, Robson walked in and was relieved to see us all in one piece because he had heard so many different stories of what had happened he expected to see bits and pieces everywhere. After the doc had checked us over we could see the relief in his face.

The doctor then took us down to the mess and gave us all a large navy rum. It tasted like shit but it did the job and calmed us all down.

There was no training for us that day so Robson arranged for us to be driven home. As the other players lived in digs I had asked them round to my house. Maggie was at work so we decided to get stuck into the lagers I had in the fridge. When she came home we were all a bit worse for the wear and she hit the roof.

"What are you lot doing here?".

I told her we had all be put on the transfer list because we were pissed off with the club. Maggie soon realised it was a joke because she knew I would never want to leave Ipswich. To this day, I cannot believe that no-one was hurt because when I went to see the car the next day it was a write-off. The roof was flat against the body with a small hole at the back where we must have squeezed through.

After the crash it was back to work and after a few more days at H.M.S. Ganges we were off to Holland to continue our preparations for the start of the season. Zeist is a small town in Holland which houses a magnificent sports centre where the Dutch national side train. I can see why the Dutch produce such great players with places like that to train. It just helps to bring out the best in you and this was to be our home for a week. We played a couple of matches in addition to plenty of hard training.

The night before we were due to come home the boss said we could go out for a drink as long as we were home by 10.30 p.m. Say no more, we got togged up and ordered the taxis and hit the town. Zeist is a small place, as I have said, so when you get fifteen or so professional footballers about news travels fast and by the time we knew it, the bar we were in was full and we were downing the drinks as though there was no tomorrow.

We had all been dry all week and a few of the lads moved on so the big man, Allan Hunter, decided to take on all comers at darts. We were playing trebles and Big Al, David Best and myself were beating the arses off everyone. The losers were buying the drinks and before we knew, the time was 10.20 p.m. We knew we had better get back or the gaffer would have our guts for garters, but we couldn't get a cab so we borrowed some bikes and off we went.

Well, if you had seen eight professional footballers pissed out of their brains on bikes it is a sight for sore eyes. For a start there were no brakes on the bikes and to stop them you had to pedal backwards, but we didn't know that. Don't forget, we were well oiled and a couple of us went through hedges and got cow shit all over us. It was like a circus. We just could not stop laughing and banging into each other.

We finally got back to the gates of the complex half an hour late and we could see Cyril Lea, our coach, waiting at the front door of the sports centre.

Now Cyril was not someone to be messed about with and when he says "jump", you said, "how high Cyril", but he always got the best out of us and if I was involved with a club, Cyril would be the first man on my list to have as a coach because he has a great knowledge of football and gets all the players respect.

Anyway we all darted off in different directions into the trees that surrounded the complex. Cyril started shouting.

"Come on you lot, I know you are out there somewhere".

Nobody made a sound and I managed somehow to get past Cyril and into my room. I got undressed and stuck my head out of the window. Cyril was just below me.

"What's the matter?", I said.

Well, if you could have seen the look on Cyril's face.

He said "Where is the big man Beat?"

I said "Big Al's asleep. We have been in bed about an hour and you woke me up shouting".

"Shit", he said, "I thought you were all out here".

Then all of a sudden the big man, who was hiding behind a tree, decided he wanted to be an owl. The thing was this owl had an Irish accent. Well, I just started to laugh it was so funny.

Cyril took one look at me and said, "Right, I'll sort you lot out in the morning".

The next morning after breakfast Cyril got us all in his room and gave us one hell of a bollocking. Then he got the kit out and ran and ran us until we all threw up and sweated all the drink out of us that we had had the night before. We were never late again.

Pre-season training means a lot of long distance running, and it was never one of my biggest attributes. Give me a short sprint and I would beat anybody. Trevor Whymark, Allan Hunter and myself used to hate long runs. The big man and I used to take our fags with us and when everybody was out of sight we would stop and have a drag. On one of the runs we used to do at Ganges, you had to run up a very steep hill at the finish, and the last player to arrive had to do an extra lap of the field.

Towards the end of one particular run I knew that Big Al was behind me so that meant no extra running for me. As I was struggling up the hill a milk float passed and sitting on the back was Allan, smoking a cigarette with a big smile on his face, like a Cheshire cat. I just collapsed and just couldn't stop laughing. So that meant an extra lap for me and when I got back to the changing rooms, Allan said:

"You have to use your brains in this game Beat".

On another occasion a few days later, we had to do a twelve minute run and I decided to go for it and went hell for leather so there was a big gap, but as the time went on the lads started to overtake me and Cyril shouted:

"One minute to go boys, keep up the good work".

I knew Trevor Whymark was a hell of a long way behind me so no problems and no extra laps. When Cyril shouted time, everybody collapsed and the boss came up to me and said.

"Come on Beat, an extra lap".

"Not me, Boss", Trevor is miles behind.

The Gaffer then said Trevor had fainted in the heat and was being looked after by the physio. I thought, fainted, it was not that hot. Here I go again, an extra lap. When I got back to the changing rooms, Trevor was sat in the bath laughing his head off.

"That's twice this week you've been caught Beat".

I had the last laugh, I hid Trevor's pants and socks and let his car tyres down. Mind you, I would give my right arm to be able to do those extra laps today.

12

Big Al and me

The partnership I forged with Allan Hunter at the heart of the Ipswich defence in their hey-day was considered by many to be the best in the country. At Derby County they talked about Roy McFarland and Colin Todd as a great central defensive partnership, but if it had gone to a vote, I reckon Allan and I would have won!

I was in the reserves when Allan was signed from Blackburn Rovers for £70,000 in a deal which took Bobby Bell the other way. Allan, already a seasoned international with Northern Ireland, soon became a big hit with the supporters at Portman Road and his influence definitely rubbed off on me. At the start of the following season when I stepped up to the first team we soon became the best of friends. Our goalkeeper David Best was a near neighbour of mine and he was also a big mate of Allan's as they used to play together at Oldham Athletic.

Besty and Big Al took me under their wing and we soon became known as the three Amigos. I used to call Besty, "dad", and Al, "uncle". On away trips we used to share a room. The night before a game I used to clean their shoes, make the tea and ring up for the papers. Derek Jefferson was Allan's partner at central defence when I first got into the team, but by early September, Jefferson had been sold to Wolves and I moved from left-back alongside Allan.

It was the start of a partnership that was to get better and better over the years. Allan was a real character and an outstanding player into the bargain. The strength of our partnership was that Allan had the knowledge and the experience and I had the power and the pace. The big man was a tremendous help right from the start. If I did something wrong during a game he would give me some stick, but I found it was difficult to talk back to him because he was an international, but if he made a mistake he would expect me to have a go at him. One incident stands out in my mind to this day. It was the F.A. Cup semi-final against West Bromwich Albion at Highbury in 1978. We were leading 2-0 and looking comfortably set to book our place at Wembley when Allan, for no apparent reason, handled the ball in the penalty area. I had a real go at him for letting Albion back into the match and all he could say was that he didn't know why he did it. In fact, he doesn't know to this day why he handled the ball.

Our partnership continued to gel in those early days and we became inseparable on and off the pitch. Our understanding on the park became telepathic and later we were christened "Eggs and Bacon" by Bobby Robson. Away from football we went everywhere together. If one of us was asked to open a shop or attend a fete, both of us went along. We regularly attended supporters' functions and if things were a bit quiet, Allan and I got up on the stage and that broke the ice.

Ipswich continued to have success both at home and abroad and I would like to think that Allan and I played a big part by giving the team a solid foundation at the back. Allan could never be intimidated on the pitch. He was his own man and opposing forwards seldom got the better of him, but at times he was so unorthodox which led to little Laurie Sivell, who had taken over in goal when David Best left the club, calling him the "strange man".

The biggest cheer during a game came when Allan booted the ball over the stand. He had to do it at least once every match at Portman Road because the fans demanded it. Everything about our partnership was more or less down to a fine art. We were always the first two at the ground for training which might surprise some people. We used to get changed then go and sit in the groundsman's hut for a cup of tea, and a cigarette. That was our routine. Neither of us were the best of trainers, we both preferred playing, and in the end injuries were to catch up with us.

By 1978 injuries had taken their toll. I didn't play many games that season while Allan was struggling with a knee injury. I know I should not have played in the F.A. Cup Final.

Allan only just made the final, having a fitness test on the

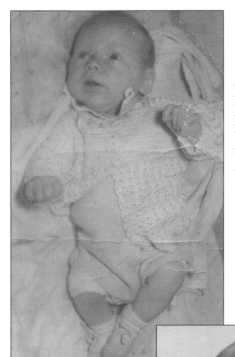

(left):
Here I am at the very
young age of just seven
weeks old. A picture
taken in February 1954.
A good looking bugger!

(right):
Nine years on and my
appearance has
changed somewhat.
What about the
wingnuts?

(left):
Now I admit that this is not the best picture in the world, but here I am with my best mate Semmie (Steven Ullrich), aged 13, in our best tableclothes.

(above):
The second best football team in the world on that day, the St Cuthberts School team for the 1964-65 season.
(Back row, left to right): Tully, Murray, Mr Rafferty, Farry, Cummins, O'Mahoney. (front, left to right): Brown, Andrews, Beattie, Rafferty, McAlindon, Hamilton.

Here I am in my first Ipswich Town shirt.

(above): July 1990, and I once again meet Bobby Robson at a reception in Ipswich Town Hall. Oh, by the way that is, my wife, Maggie doing her best to obscure me.

(left):
Bobby Robson is welcomed at Ipswich Station by the legendary Mr John Cobbold in January 1969 upon his appointment as the club's manager.

(above): Had I been injured at the time and laying on Wembley's lush turf then this is the view I might have got of Roger Osborne scoring that goal against Arsenal, but luckily for once I had both feet firmly on the ground.

(below): Look what we've won. Mick Mills has his hand on the Cup, but Paul Mariner has his on the bottle. I won't tell you where his other hand is!

(above): What a moment to savour, three Carlisle lads, Rob
Turner, Dave Geddis and yours truly, revelling in the
adulation as we parade the F.A. Cup around Wembley
Stadium. By the way, Paul Cooper sneaked in too.
(below): To get to Wembley we had to overcome the stern
challenge set by West Bromwich Albion at Highbury. Here I
appear to be controlling the ball with my chin!
Unlucky Cyrille!

(above): Big Al, Allan Hunter, and I go looking for a fag
during the F.A. Cup Final victory over Arsenal.
I don't think it was even half time because everyone
else is going in the opposite direction.

The Homecoming: On the steps of the Corn Exchange with
the Mayor and Mayoress of Ipswich in attendance.
Check out the bell-bottoms!!

The locks are shorn for this picture taken soon after the
filming of Escape To Victory had been completed.
I was Michael Caine's "double" in the movie.
Not a lot of people know that.

My daughter Emma proudly displays my England cap
awarded for a match against Scotland.

(above): Training at Wembley Stadium with Bob Latchford, Alan Ball and Malcolm Macdonald. In the background Terry McDermott was checking out the dog traps with Les Cocker.

(left): Big Al and I enjoying the sunshine whilst with Ipswich Town in Barcelona.

Now when they said my new sponsored form of transport
had arrived at Portman Road I thought I was getting a new
car. I have to say that I needed a bigger "weapon" judging
by the tighness of my strides!!

So who is getting the round in?
Kjell and I get to grips with a bar in Norway.

Away to Carlisle, no problem for most of the team as
(left to right) David Geddis, myself, Robin Turner and
Steve McCall all herald from that fair city.

78

My time at Barnet was all too brief but during this period I was able to link up with two footballing "legends". Barry Fry (above) was the manager, and, (right), Mr Stan Flashman, the chairman and well-known entrepreneur. Especially around the time when the F.A. Cup Final tickets went on sale.

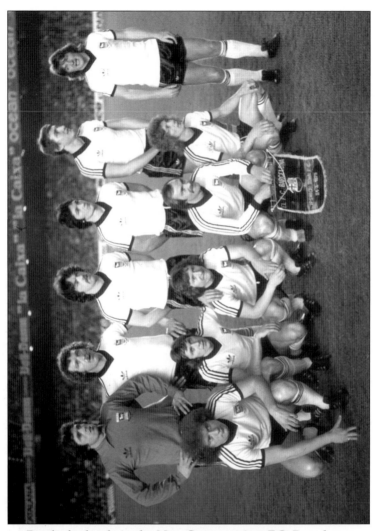

Ready for battle in the Nou Camp against F.C. Barcelona.
The Ipswich Town F.C. starting line-up that evening was:
(standing) (l-r): Paul Cooper, myself, John Wark, George
Burley, Terry Butcher, Russell Osman.
(crouching) Alan Brazil, with bird's nest on top of his head, I
have noticed that he does not wear it anymore, Arnold
Mühren, Eric Gates, Mick Mills and Clive Woods.

morning of the game. Early on in the final against Arsenal, I knocked a ball square to Mick Mills which did not impress the Big Man. He told me to get the ball forward as quickly as possible because we didn't want it at the back!

Many people have never been quite sure how to take Allan, but let me assure you he has a heart of gold. I shall never forget when I was laying at death's door in 1991 how supportive the he was to me. Every night he used to visit me in hospital with his wife Carol. One night I remember he took me down to the day room and trimmed my moustache and generally could not do enough for me.

One or two incidents stand out during our career at Portman Road. The 1974-75 season was one, but for the wrong reasons. There was an unfortunate incident during our home game against Stoke City when their big striker John Ritchie broke his leg in a tackle with me. It was a 50-50 challenge, but because of my power it was the ball that broke his leg. After the game I went into the Stoke dressing room to find out how he was, but was told that he had already gone to hospital. As it turned out he stayed in hospital overnight before going home to Stoke, but I did not know this. Later that day their manager, Tony Waddington, had a right go at me in public, saying that it was disgraceful that I had made no effort to go and see Ritchie. Had I known that he was still in hospital in Ipswich I would have been up their straightaway. In the return match at Stoke later in the season Dennis Smith, their central defender, also broke his leg, this time in a challenge with Big Al. Again it was a 50-50 challenge and no blame could be attached to the Big Man. It was an accident pure and simple, just like mine was against Ritchie, but those incidents were not forgotten as far as Stoke were concerned, and in particular Tony Waddington.

Before our game at the Victoria Ground the following season, which incidentally we won 1-0, Waddington went at lengths to stir things up. Allan and I were targets for the crowd. They booed us every time we touched the ball and coins were thrown from the terraces.

It got so bad that at one point the referee stopped the game and had a word with the police with a result that a tannoy announcement was made telling the crowd to stop throwing missiles. After the match we went as usual to the players lounge for a drink, but right away I sensed there was an atmosphere. I left first and got on to the bus when I spotted my dad waiting to have a word with me. As I went to speak to him three Stoke supporters came up to me and said they wanted to fight me. Things were beginning to get out of hand when big Al appeared. Almost immediately some more Stoke fans gathered near the bus with the intent of sorting out Allan and myself. The biggest of them was holding the hand of a child, but still wanted a fight. Allan told him to take the child home and then come back to sort it out. Within seconds the child had been given to someone else before Al put the Stoke fan on the ground with a big punch. After that the rest of the Stoke supporters who had been after our blood dispersed.

Big Al said to me, "If you knock the biggest one down, the rest won't want to know."

That taught me a valuable lesson as how to handle a situation like that. Everything had been sorted out so quickly. Allan may have been soft at heart, but he was a hard man when he wanted to be. Even to this day Stoke fans hate us. It is one place I never wanted to go after that, but the blame must be firmly put at Tony Waddington's door.

I felt sorry for Mick Mills when he went there as manager because some of their fans were still talking about it all those years later.

Another example of Allan Hunter was after a match at Newcastle. We were travelling by train and had to change at Darlington. While waiting for our connection, Allan and I had a stroll along the platform when we bumped into some very rowdy Newcastle supporters. One of the group had a verbal go at big Al and within seconds it had turned into a scrap. One of the group jumped on him and as I went to help him I noticed the rest of our players boarding the train which had just pulled in. Queen's Park Rangers had been playing at Middlesbrough and were on the train. Phil Parkes, their goalkeeper, saw what was happening and came and gave us a bit of help. The incident was soon over and we boarded the train, but what shocked me and Phil was that none of the other players from both teams came to our rescue. Soon afterwards Allan thanked me for sticking by him, but he was my mate and that was the least I could do. His words meant so much to me.

I remember a match against Manchester City at Maine Road when Allan hadn't given Brian Kidd, now Alex Ferguson's assistant at Manchester United, a look-in but I nearly ended up with a serious injury. Kidd had been moaning all the match that he could not get any change out of the Big Man. During the second half I went up for a corner and just before the kick was taken, instinct told me something was going to happen. Kidd's elbow missed me by a whisker, and had it caught me I reckon it could have put me out of action for a long time. I turned round and said something to Kidd and he was surprised it was me. He thought I was Allan and after that it put him off his game completely.

13

The Beattie Tank

It was a sunny morning at the start of the 1975/76 season when I got to the ground and the boss came up to me and said he wanted to see me after training.

What the hell this time, I thought. We had a long training session and afterwards I sat in the bath trying to think what I had done wrong for him to call me into his office.

Well after stalling for about an hour, I said to myself "right let's get it over with" and I went up to see him.

I knocked on the door, and he shouted "come in".

When I got into his office he was sat behind his desk with a big smile on his face.

He said, "Sit down son, I have some good news for you. The British Army have named a tank after you". I had been named the Daily Mirror Footballer of the Month.

"Bloody hell, are you taking the piss boss?" I said.

"No son, that is the truth".

What had happened was the boys from the Tank Corps in Germany had watched me on the box and I had picked up the nickname of "The Tank" from my runs up the field. So they asked the Commander if they could call a Chieftain Tank after me.

He said "O.K." and they brought it over to the ground at Portman Road.

"That's great boss. What do I have to do?".

"They are bringing it into the ground today, and I want you to have photos taken with it".

The tank was on a trailer when it got to the ground and it was so big it would not go through the main gates. There were T.V. people and reporters everywhere.

"How the hell do you know about this?" I asked them.

"We have known for two or three days Beat," they said.

"Bloody marvellous", I said. "Always the last to know".

Well I didn't really mind and the Boss had kept it quiet so that he could see the surprise on my face. I had some photos taken and received a plaque from the Commander. It was a great moment in my life and I was a real proud man.

I even got the chance to drive it when I went to Germany to present the medals after their annual game of football between the Army and the Navy in Münchengladbach.

The day after the game I went to the tank range and they kitted me up with all the gear and there she was, the Beattie Tank with twelve inch letters on the side.

Boy was I pleased.

They gave me a few lessons and then let me drive it on my own. It was great. Here I was with fifty tons of fighting machine under me and it was so graceful and smooth. I took it onto the assault course and had a great day. I hadn't had as much fun in a long time and I would like to thank everybody involved. They really made me feel special.

14

The Highs

When I look back over my career there were, of course, some big disappointments. Having to finish too early because of injuries is the obvious one, but there are a host of memories I will always treasure.

1972-73: It was my first full season. Making my debut at Old Trafford on the opening day of the season was very special, and we ended the campaign finishing fourth in the First Division and qualifying for Europe. In addition we won the Texaco Cup, beating our old rivals Norwich City 4-2 on aggregate. To make the season complete, I was voted Player of the Year.

1973-74: I didn't miss a game! The run we had in the UEFA Cup was exciting, but ended in disappointment when we were knocked out at the quarter-final stage by Lokomotiv Leipzig. The highlight was playing against Real Madrid in the first round.

I shall never forget our match against Lazio in Rome. It was without doubt the most frightening game of my life and so intimidating for the players and the fans. I'll always remember that when Colin Viljoen scored a penalty he then had to race the length of the pitch and hide behind our goalkeeper David Best. Even before the match the Lazio supporters tried to disrupt us. A crowd gathered outside our hotel hooting horns and trying disturb us, but our doctor had given us sleeping pills and we never heard a thing!

The memories of Leipzig are still vivid today. Mick Mills, who had been sent off in the first half, was crying in the dressing room and Allan Hunter having to take that sudden-death penalty. He didn't want to take it, but being the professional he was, didn't duck out.

1974-75: There was high hopes of two cup fronts, but we fell in the closing stages. In the League Cup, Norwich City knocked us out in a fifth round replay at Portman Road, and Johnny Miller, who had left us and signed for the Canaries only a month earlier, scored both their goals.

However, it was in the F.A. Cup that was the real sickener. Wembley was well within our sights for what would have been our first ever final appearance when referee Clive Thomas virtually ended those hopes in our semi-final replay against West Ham at Stamford Bridge.

Thomas disallowed what was a perfectly good goal from Bryan Hamilton and a year or so later admitted he had made a mistake. Had it been allowed to stand I am convinced we would have gone and beaten the Hammers. After our thrilling quarter-final victory over Leeds United at the fourth attempt I was certain we would go all the way. I didn't play in the third replay because of injury with a young John Wark taking my place. I watched from the stands, but could not have been more delighted when Clive Woods scored that wonderful winning goal.

1975-76: The lasting memory of that season was the UEFA Cup defeat by Bruges of Belgium. We had won the first leg 3-0 at Portman Road, but then lost the second leg 4-0. Nine times out of ten I would have played with the help of an injection, but Bobby Robson wouldn't let me because he felt that we had done enough in the first leg to go through.

1976-77: The season we came very close to winning the First Division Championship. Then I had my bonfire accident and missed the last seven games. Whether my absence made a difference we'll never know.

1977-78: Indifferent form in the league. but of course winning the F.A. Cup made for all that. Robin Turner's two goals against Bristol Rovers at Eastville certainly kept us on the Wembley trail. Robin missed out on the final which is well documented in another chapter.

1978 79: We were back at Wembley for the F.A. Charity Shield, a week before the start of the season, but with so many players out through injury we were well beaten, 5-0, by Nottingham Forest, the League Champions. I remember Allan Hunter and Paul Mariner watched the game on television in a pub near the ground. It was an on off season as far as I was concerned because of injuries and I only played in the big games. One of them was the Cup Winners Cup tie against Barcelona in Spain which we lost on penalties.

1979-80: Things had gone from bad to worse as far as I was concerned. My career was going downhill because of injuries. I was frightened to see the specialist because I knew what he was going to say. At 27 I should have been in my prime, but deep down I knew I was finished. I wasn't able to train and played only the odd game and suffered for it with my knee.

1980-81: We should have won the F.A. Cup as well as the UEFA Cup. The F.A. Cup semi-final against Manchester City at Villa Park when we lost to Paul Power's extra time free kick, proved to be my last game for the club. Injury struck again, but this time it was a broken arm that forced me to go off before the end. In the UEFA Cup I was mainly on the substitutes' bench. I came on and scored in the tie against Bohemians of Prague at Portman Road and remember I was the only player to wear a short-sleeved shirt in the return leg in freezing temperatures.

Before the second leg of the UEFA Cup Final, I fell out with Bobby Robson. Although my arm was still in plaster from the F.A. Cup semi-final injury, I felt he could have included me amongst the five substitutes. Robson refused and as a result I never got a medal. I thought I deserved one if only for my goal against Bohemians which turned out to be vital. I was really upset about it. Radio Orwell, the local station, asked me if I would help out, but it wasn't the same and I found it difficult to join in the celebrations afterwards.

1981-82: I was finished with Ipswich Town and my next stop was Colchester United. I only went there because my old mate Allan Hunter was manager. Charlie Simpson, their physiotherapist, got my knee right again. It took a long time and I only played three games for Colchester before Malcolm Allison signed me for Middlesbrough. Malcolm was the greatest coach I had come across and he made me captain. He always used to consult me over the picking of the team and in fact I picked it myself on a couple of occasions!

I remember we used to do ballet dancing as part of our training. However, after one season I left when Malcolm got the sack. I became disillusioned because I felt the club was going nowhere. I came back to Ipswich and played for Harwich and Parkeston in the Eastern Counties League.

There were many memorable matches during my career, but two of them were European matches with Ipswich Town.

The first one was on September 17th, 1975 when we went to Holland for a first round, first leg, match against Feyenoord and came away with a 2-1 victory.

Feyenoord had been made the favourites to win the competition but we gave an outstanding display. What sticks out in my memory was the awful weather conditions, as it lashed down with rain throughout the match.

The other match that has fond memories is the one in March 1981 when we played St. Etienne in the quarter-finals of the UEFA Cup.

The first leg was in France with St. Etienne, the red hot favourites, which was not surprising considering they had not been beaten at home in European competition in the previous years.

I knew were going to win that match even before a ball was kicked. When the two teams were waiting in the tunnel before going on to the pitch, I looked into the eyes of the St. Etienne players. I could tell that they were nervous and there was a definite look of lack of confidence, and so it proved. We went out and beat them 4-1 in one of the most outstanding performances by any team playing in Europe.

We went on to defeat the French giants 7-2 on aggregate and eventually lifted the UEFA Cup two months later in Amsterdam, but that night in St. Etienne was definitely something very special.

1982 was to be a big year for me and also a sad one. It was to be my testimonial year. It was a privilege to be given a testimonial by the club you have played for and normally happens after you have served them for ten years. The club had also given, in previous years, a testimonial to Bobby Robson and big Allan Hunter.

Anyway when I heard the news I got myself a committee which were a very good team of people. The most important event was the actual game and the committee arranged for Dynamo Kiev, who were led by the greatest of all goalkeepers,

Lev Yashin, to come to England to play. Lev was acting as ambassador for the club.

Mind you I was very lucky to get them. Ron Greenwood, the England manager, was going to bring an England team to play, but at the last moment had to cancel. Dynamo Kiev had a game cancelled and one the committee members found out about it. He got on the phone and booked them up straight away at a cost of £7,000. It was expensive at the time and I thought the Ipswich public deserved to see them. Sod the price, the supporters deserved the best.

The team was staying at the Post House Hotel just on the outskirts of Ipswich, so when they arrived I went along to see them. The players were all in their rooms, so my committee and the great Mr John Cobbold were looking after the staff and Lev Yashin. They had been with them a few hours by the time I got to the hotel and they had put a few drinks away.

Bob Shelley was on the committee and gave Lev Yashin a crate of whisky for a present. You would have thought we had given him a gold bar as he was kissing everyone and thanking them, even the girls who were serving him got a kiss. That was a kick start Mr John was waiting for, as he also started kissing everyone. The pair of them were going round the hotel kissing and hugging everyone who was there.

It was so funny and after a while we sat down and started to talk. Lev invited Mr John to go to Russia. He took up the offer a few years later and brought me back a bottle of vodka that blew my head off.

The game itself was fantastic. There were 17,000 people at Portman Road that evening and I ran out with my eldest daughter, Emma, who was my mascot for the evening. I received a fantastic reception. Looking back, the testimonial was up there with the F.A. Cup final reception we received at the Cornhill and it made me quite humble that all these people had turned out especially for my testimonial game.

The game ended 2-2 and I did a lap of honour at the end. I could see grown men crying in the stands and it was therefore a happy and sad night as I knew deep down that my days as a Town player were running out.

I do love the Town supporters. They mean so much to me

and my family, but at the end of the 1982 season I was finally
told I had to pack up in football.

15

End of Season Tours

The life of a professional footballer, especially for those playing at the top level, is a great one. Being paid for something you enjoy and the chance to visit some of the best places in the world.

During my time at Ipswich the club went on several close season tours to exotic places I had only previously read about in magazines. One trip that sticks out in my mind was one to Bermuda. Let me say right away that I hate flying and by the time we landed at New York on route to the Caribbean I was a bag of nerves. If I had not had plenty to drink on the leg between England and America I don't think I would have got on the plane to Bermuda. By the time we reached Bermuda I literally staggered off the plane into the searing heat.

Our hotel was on a golf course about ten minutes from the sea and we were sleeping three to a room. My room mates were Eric Gates and John Peddelty.

After playing and beating a local team we had ten days holiday and that was the time to see the sights. "Gatesy" and "Spock", as John Peddelty was known, and me found a quiet little beach and armed with cans of lager decided on a day of relaxation, or so we thought. The first crisis came when Gatesy was paddling and slipped into a hole out of his depth. I got hold of him and he was in a real state. He had panicked because he could not swim.

A few hours later we had to go back for a meeting with Bobby Robson and arriving at the hotel we went straight to our room, took one look in the mirror and saw the colour of our skin. We looked like tomatoes. Now Robson always had the habit of repeating himself and as the meeting dragged on I started to feel ill. I looked across the room and Gatesy was even worse. Straight after the meeting we rushed to our room and

Gatesy and I were sick. We realised we had caught sunstroke and were confined to bed for the next couple of days. Spock had obviously been more careful and escaped our fate.

Once we recovered we wanted to make up for lost time. I was introduced to a policeman who was a friend of Ian Collard, one of the players on the trip. He offered us the chance to go scuba diving and Ian, myself, Spock, and several of the lads decided to have a go. Having made sure the gear was in order and that there was plenty of lagers on board the speedboat, off we went to a spot about five miles off-shore.

Into the water we dived only to see a shadow of a ship. I could not get back onto the speedboat quick enough. On the plane to New York they had showed a film called "The Deep", the story about divers and a monster eel. I took some ribbing about not wanting to go scuba diving and whilst the rest were underwater I sat on deck and drank the afternoon away. In the evening, our policeman friend took Ian and myself out on the town. Among our various visits to watering holes we had cocktails in a cruise ship that had stopped off in Bermuda.

The Captain, as it turned out, was an Ipswich Town supporter and he told me he had seen me play for England.

Next morning I woke to see stripes in front of my eyes. My head was exploding with black and white stripes. That was something else. I then realised I was in a jail cell and in the other corner was Ian. Soon afterwards our policeman friend came along to tell us that we had been so drunk he'd locked us up for the night to make sure we didn't get into trouble. He then gave us a slap up breakfast before taking us back to our hotel.

In subsequent years I enjoyed many other trips to all corners of the world including the one to Martinique, a French Island in the Caribbean. As on all the other trips we had to play a game and the rest of the time was our own.

We played the waiters from all the hotels on the Island and gave them a good hiding. Myself, and colleagues, Terry Austin, Mick Mills and Eric Gates were in one room and I said, "let's wind up Spock.".

So I telephoned his room and said it was Harry Miller from the Daily Mirror. I actually said it the wrong way round. "It's Harry Mirror from the Miller".

"Hello Harry" said John "What can I do for you?".

"Right" I said. "I understand you are playing well and hope to take either the place of Beattie or Hunter next season".

"Yes I am," said John, "I think I have a great chance of playing because I am better than them".

Well after a while I said, "Can you hold on a minute?".

"O.K." said John.

I put my hand over the phone as me and the rest of the boys were pissing ourselves laughing and I had to tell the boys to keep quiet. In the end they had to go on the balcony so Spock couldn't hear them.

"Right John," I said. "We have a photographer on the Island so can he come and take some shots of you?".

"Fine," said John. "What time will it be?".

"It will be sometime early evening," I said.

"O.K. I'll be ready," said John.

"Thanks," I said in my best London accent.

The next thing was to hide the boys as I knew Spock would come up to my room and tell me. Sure enough there was a knock on the door and Spock ran in to tell me everything.

"Bloody great," I said. "Is there any cash in it, and if there is I hope you buy the lads a drink".

"No problems," said Spock, and he left the room to get ready for his interview and his picture. The lads were in stitches.

We had a night out that evening. When we got down to the hotel lobby there was Spock in his best clobber sitting in reception.

"What time is he coming?", I said.

"About eight," said Spock. "So I'll catch up with you later".

We could not keep our faces straight so we dashed out of the hotel. We had a great night and got back to the hotel about one o'clock in the morning and there was Spock still sitting there.

"Well," I said, "what's happened?".

"No bother," said Spock. "He has rung to say he would be a little bit late, so I thought I'd just hang on".

We all went up and had a few drinks in our room and I decided to put Spock out of his misery, so I phoned the lobby and asked for Mr Peddelty.

"This is the photographer from the Daily Mirror. I am so

sorry to say I have left for England because there is a big story I have to do".

"O.K." said John. "No problems. I will phone you when I get back to England and perhaps we can arrange something".

I couldn't contain myself any further and a few minutes later Spock knocked on my door. A few of the boys were having a sandwich and a beer.

"Well, what happened mate?".

"Yes, he has just left me. Should be in the newspapers next week".

To this day he still doesn't know what happened and when he reads this I hope he'll see the funny side because he is now a policeman. Thanks John, you gave the lads a great laugh and you are a star mate.

One other little story to tell is that when we went abroad, our physio Brian Simpson used to give out a little box with things in like sunburn cream, calamine lotion, headache pills and other things if we got ill. Well one day, Bobby Ferguson had the shits and asked Brian for something to help.

Brian said: "I have something in my room that will help. It is in a brown bottle so go up and get it".

Bobby rushed up to Brian's room and took something. The next day Fergie did not look well and asked Brian why. Brian asked him to go to his room so he could have a look. When Brian got down he was pissing himself.

"What's the joke?" asked the lads.

"You know Bob had the jitters last night. Well he took the wrong stuff, instead of taking Kaolin and Morphine he took Calamine Lotion".

"What will happen to him Brian?" we said.

"Nothing, but he will be shitting Milky Bars for a couple of days".

We pissed ourselves with laughter and Fergie was thereafter known as the Milky Bar Kid.

End of season tours were always a reward for a long hard season and time to let your hair down, and as you can see I certainly did that.

16

Beat in the Movies!!

Have you ever fancied being a film star? I have in my dreams, but they turned into reality in 1981.

Bobby Robson called the first team players into a meeting one day earlier that year and introduced us to a film producer called Freddie Fields. I must confess that none of us had heard of him, but once he started talking he quickly gained our attention.

Freddie and John Huston – yes, I'd heard of him – were to make a film set in a prisoner of war camp in Germany with the English POW's taking on the German national side at soccer. He told us that the game was a plot to cover the POW's escape, and that many of our players would be suitable for various parts in the film.

Freddie said that Michael Caine and Sylvester Stallone would have the starring roles with Tim Piggot-Smith and Max von Saddow, the co-stars, and he had already signed up Bobby Moore, Mike Summerbee, Ossie Ardiles and Pele.

So where did we come in? Freddie said that he had watched a few of our games recently and had the players whom he considered would fit into the script.

Russell Osman, John Wark, Kevin O'Callaghan, Robin Turner and Laurie Sivell would play Germans, and that we thought, was that. Then Freddie announced that Paul Cooper would play understudy to Stallone and that I would do the same for Michael Caine. You could have knocked me down with a feather.

The film was to be made in Budapest, Hungary that summer and as far as "Coop" and I were concerned, we would wear masks so that we would pass for the stars. For "Coop" and me it was off to London for a fitting of our masks. That was easier said than done. I sat down and a chap put Vaseline on my hair, explaining it was to stop the plaster sticking to me.

He then mixed some plaster and poured it all over my hair and face. It was a great feeling until it covered my mouth and I found I couldn't breathe. He told me to breathe through my nose, but that wasn't easy as I had broken my nose so many times, and even to this day I find breathing difficult.

I had to have a couple of pipes stuck up my nose so the mask could be put on, and Maggie and the kids, who had travelled with me to London, sat there laughing. I must have been quite a sight, It wasn't a very pleasant experience and a little later I had to go through it all again because the first mask had not come out the way it should have done.

A fortnight later and we were off to Hungary. Freddie wanted to get the shooting of the match completed before the weather broke, and on our arrival in Budapest we were taken straight to the stadium to start filming. The first person I saw was Robin Turner with his hair cut very short. He told me that everyone in the film had to have his hair cut in this way, and that didn't please me.

Mine was shoulder length and in any case I didn't particularly like having my hair cut. Then it was off to meet Michael Caine. He had a private caravan on the set, and I was a bit nervous to say the least, but I need not have worried. He made me very welcome and I had to pinch myself that I was sitting chatting to one of the biggest film stars in the world as though I had known him for years.

Then it was time to have my hair cut and it was Michael's personal hairdresser that did it. I hardly recognised myself once he had finished with the scissors! Now the real work started. Mike Summerbee came up to me and said: "Hullo Michael. Where is the Beat?" I told him to stop taking the piss, but he told me that I was the spitting image of Michael Caine.

I went over to see how "Coop" was getting on with Sylvester Stallone, but he wasn't. "Coop" told me that Stallone had said in no uncertain terms that he didn't want him as his understudy. Mind you, Stallone still wanted "Coop" to teach him how to dive properly as a goalkeeper does. From what I saw, Stallone might have been a star actor, but he was an awful goalkeeper and an arrogant sod into the bargain.

The weather was boiling hot, made worse because we had khaki uniforms on, and the days were very long. We had to be up by 5am and didn't finish filming until some thirteen hours later.

After filming it was back to the hotel for dinner. I simply loved the Hungarian goulash and ate it every night. After dinner we'd have a few beers before going to bed exhausted.

Sometimes Michael Caine and his wife joined us for a drink, but we never saw Stallone. He even stayed in a different hotel to the rest of us.

Despite the long days, it was great fun. One day Michael Caine came up to me and asked me for a favour. He wanted me to kick a big bloke on the other side because he couldn't catch him. The big bloke was, in fact, the Hungarian weightlifting champion who stood 6' 5" and looked as broad as he was tall. All I will say is this. The Hungarian didn't finish the film and Michael was very happy.

One night we had a good drinking session and when we came down the next morning, Bobby Moore and Mike Summerbee were still at the bar. They were in no fit state to do any filming that day, so it was decided to do the scene where Pele scores with a great overhead kick. That was something special. Pele was supposed to have a broken arm and returned to the game later after being carried off. With his first shot he scored with an amazing shot and Laurie Sivell, who was the German goalkeeper, could not believe it.

John Huston and Freddie Fields wanted Pele to do it again, but despite trying half a dozen times, he couldn't beat Laurie. It was then decided that the first shot would be the one used in the actual film.

Pele was an amazing man even years after packing up playing. One day he got an orange and juggled it on his feet, head and shoulders for at least ten minutes.

When the filming was over it was time to go home, but I shall never forget the experience.

It was a privilege to take part in the film, which has been shown on television many times, with so many stars. The biggest star to my mind was Bobby Moore. Even though he has died, I will never forget him. He was a great amongst men.

Sylvester Stallone, on the other had, was entirely different. He was really full of himself. When there was a break during the filming he would take off his shirt and show off his huge frame.

He was only a small man, about five foot eight inches, but his upper body was twice the size of everybody else. He would show off by doing arm push-ups in front of everyone. There was not an ounce of fat on him and he had this huge scar on the side of his torso from his armpit nearly to his waist. I asked him how he did it, and he told me that when he was training for one of the Rocky films, his skin was so tight that he hit the punch bag and the skin split and the muscle actually popped out.

The lads were all winding him up that I had a fair body myself, and had never been beaten at arm wrestling with my left arm. Stallone came up and challenged me to an arm wrestle. I said, "you have got to be joking", looking at the size of his arms to mine. The lads got me to take the challenge and we had a bet of £100 for the best of three, one right arm, one left arm and if it was a draw we would toss a coin and the winner picked his best arm.

We started with the left and I won. He won the right and so the coin was tossed. I shouted tails and tails it was and, of course, I picked my left. He was not a happy man as although it was harder that time, the Beat came shining through and Stallone was really pissed off as I got my £100 and he never spoke to me for the rest of the filming.

Apparently in all films that he appears in, the camera angle makes him look bigger, which it does. I haven't watched any of his films since Escape To Victory. He might be a multi-millionaire but he was a very arrogant bugger. Mind you, if he wanted to bet £1,000 on a rematch I would definitely give him a challenge.

Escape To Victory was not my first experience of the film industry. The first time Ipswich played Barcelona was in the third round of the UEFA Cup during the 1977-78 season.

I played in the first leg at Portman Road when we gained a sensational 3-0 victory and will always be remembered for the way Roger Osborne marked the legendary Johann Cruyff out of the game, but for the return leg a fortnight later I was out injured. Bobby Robson decided to take me to Spain to help rally the troops. He reckoned my bubbly personality would be a big help.

Despite holding a 3-0 lead, Robson was taking nothing for granted. The Nou Camp is a magnificent stadium with a capacity of more than 100,000, but because Barcelona had suffered such a big defeat at Portman Road, their fans turned their backs on the tie and the attendance was only 24,000.

On the night before the match the lads went to the Nou Camp for a training session and later over dinner, Mel Henderson, who was the Public Relations Officer at the club, said to me:

"By the way there is a film crew here at the hotel who would like an Ipswich player to have some pictures taken with a famous Spanish actress."

Robson said it was o.k. as I was not playing and I then told Mel that if he could organise everything, I would be waiting in the lounge.

The film crew said they wanted to take pictures of me with the Spanish actress sitting on my lap. There were a lot of photographers waiting to take pictures by the time everything was ready. Imagine my surprise when this woman in a long mink coat came over to me, but even more so when she took it off revealing she had nothing on but a string vest!

"What the hell's going on?", I asked Mel. He simply told me not to worry. "The pictures are only for a Spanish magazine."

When she sat on my knee I could see everything, literally. After taking a few pictures, I said: "O.K, that's enough".

Then Mel revealed that the woman was Spain's biggest porn star. I felt as though I had been stitched up and I went berserk.

"What if this appears in the English papers?", I asked Mel.

"There's no chance of that", was his reply.

The day after the match we headed for the airport to fly back to England. On the plane they had the English papers and there was a picture of me with this porn star sitting on my lap. I was furious and had a right go at Mel, but all he could say was that something must have gone wrong.

Of course, it cheered the lads up no end, but what

naturally worried me was what Maggie was going to day when I got home.

It was no great surprise that she hit the roof and in the end I had to get Mel to come round to our house to explain everything. She later cooled down, but it had been an unpleasant couple of days for me and could have landed me in really hot water.

Looking back, I can see the funny side of it all, but at the time I was really angry.

By the way love, if you get a copy of this book – what great tits you had!

17

Middlesbrough & Big Mal

I was sitting in the treatment room at Colchester United – surprise, surprise! – when Charlie Simpson, the physiotherapist, told me that there a phone call for me, and that it was Malcolm Allison from Middlesbrough.

I thought it was a wind-up by Charlie, who at the time was nursing me back to full fitness. In fact, Charlie had done wonders for my knee and I was happy being involved with the Fourth Division club, but the phone call from Malcolm Allison changed all that.

'Boro were in Division Two at the time and immediately it went through my mind if I was going to have the chance to play at a higher level, take it. But more to the point, could I still do it?

Malcolm told me that he wanted me to sign for 'Boro. He was very convincing, and at the same time, genuine, and he wanted me to go up to see him later that week. When I went home to Ipswich that night, I popped round and told my mate, Bob Shelley, about 'Boro's interest and he said he would drive me up to the north-east on the Thursday morning.

We arrived on Teesside at lunch-time and drove straight to the Baltimore Hotel where Malcolm had arranged to meet us. There were several reporters waiting because the news had already broken that I was coming to sign for 'Boro, but no sign of the man himself.

About an hour later "Big Mal" arrived and as soon as he walked into the hotel there was an aura about him. I made up my mind that I wanted to play for him. Call it instinct, or what you like, but I was convinced about it even though I had never met him before. In fact, it took only ten minutes to sort things out and when everything was completed, Malcolm ordered a bottle of champagne to celebrate.

I said that I didn't think that I should have a drink as I

thought I would be training, but Malcolm told me that 'Boro did not train in the afternoons. In any case, I was tired and said I would prefer to go to my room for a sleep.

I left Malcolm and Bob talking, but three hours later when I came down to the bar, they were on their sixth bottle of champagne and smoking huge cigars. Bob was meant to return to Ipswich that night, but he was in no fit state.

The next morning Bob headed off back to Ipswich and Malcolm took me off to Ayresome Park to meet the players and staff. The first person I bumped into was Ray Hankin. We had had some great battles in the past when he played for Burnley and Leeds and we immediately got on like a house on fire.

George Armstrong and the late Cyril Knowles were the coaches, and after meeting the players I had my first training session. Immediately afterwards, Malcolm dropped a bombshell when he told everyone that I was to be the new captain. It took me completely by surprise because Malcolm had not mentioned this earlier. I could see that Irving Nattrass was not too happy, but Malcolm qualified it by saying that I would be the team skipper and Irving the club captain.

I soon had a good rapport with my new team-mates and the fans quickly took to me. I found that strange at first because when I played at Ayresome Park in the past for Ipswich, they gave me stick.

I was given the number six shirt, the one Willie Maddren, a 'Boro legend used to wear. He was the same player that Bobby Robson tried to sign for Ipswich. As I said in earlier chapter, had Maddren agreed to come to Suffolk then I might not have got my chance.

It did not take me long to realise that Malcolm was the best coach I had ever come across, and with Knowles and Armstrong, they made a great team. To some people Malcolm's ideas might have seemed a bit far-fetched. For instance, he employed a guy named Roger to give us ballet lessons – big Ray Hankin looked like a hippo out of a Disney film! – but they worked.

Bryan "Pop" Robson, who played for Newcastle and West Ham United, was also a ballroom dancing champion and a British table tennis player. "Pop" gave us table tennis lessons designed to help our balance and centre of gravity in order to get us quicker off the mark. They certainly worked and they were ideas devised by Malcolm who, in my opinion, was years ahead of his time.

On the pitch things were going great for me. In the third round of the F.A. Cup we beat Notts County, then a First Division side, 2-1 before a full house at Ayresome Park and I scored the winner from the penalty spot. In truth we outplayed County on the day and could also afford the luxury of missing two penalties. When we were awarded a third one, I took it on myself to take it, so I picked up the ball, put it down on the spot and sent their goalkeeper the wrong way. It was a great result for Middlesbrough because they had been having a bad time before I went there. I am not trying to say that I was their saviour but perhaps it was no coincidence that they picked up after my arrival.

The next match was a local derby against Newcastle United, which had been billed as a battle of the two Kevins. My old England team-mate, Kevin Keegan, was the key player for Newcastle and the match ended in a 1-1 draw with KK scoring their goal, but with me carried off with a torn groin.

Here we go again, I thought, as though I hadn't had enough injury problems throughout my career, but this one was the worst. The 'Boro physio said he had never seen anything quite like it.

As it turned out, that was to be my last match in a 'Boro shirt. It also cost me the chance to play against my old manager Bobby Robson who had brought an England side to Ayresome Park for a benefit match for the legendary Wilf Mannion. Malcolm later told me that he had spoken to Robson at the match and said I should still be playing for England as I was as good as there was in the country.

During the close season, Malcolm worked hard reducing the financial debt at the club. Some shrewd dealings in the transfer market in addition to getting fifty blokes off the dole to paint the ground and in return, gave them season tickets. He even got the paint on the cheap from ICI.

That was typical Malcolm Allison, but his reward was the sack. I was shattered when I heard the news and decided it was time for me to leave as well. It had been a great eighteen months on Teesside, the people in the north-east were smashing, but it was time to go.

'Boro are a club whose fortunes I have always followed closely since and I am delighted Bryan Robson has got them back into the Premiership at the first attempt.

I have always been a big rock fan and while I was playing for Middlesbrough I had the chance to meet Whitesnake, one of my favourite bands of all time. David Coverdale, the lead singer, used to be with Deep Purple. He had got a fantastic voice and later teamed up with Micky Moore and Cozy Powell to form Whitesnake.

My pal Bob, who was the manager of the Baltimore Hotel, where I stayed while I was at 'Boro, was very friendly with them. After training one day Bob said he had a surprise for me but would not tell me what it was until I returned to the hotel. When I walked into the bar you could have knocked me down with a feather. Standing there were the members of one of the greatest rock groups ever.

We hit it off from the start and before they left had invited me to go and see their show in Manchester the following week. Later on, my boss, Malcolm Allison turned up at the hotel and the champagne started to flow like water.

I discovered that Whitesnake had left V.I.P. tickets for their gig at the Odeon in Manchester which happened to be on the day 'Boro played that match against Notts County at Ayresome Park in the F.A. Cup.

Following a couple of drinks in the players' lounge, Bob and I set off for Manchester for the gig. What I didn't know was that Bob had arranged everything. We arrived at a hotel and I needed to change because you don't watch Whitesnake wearing a suit.

"Where do I change?", I asked Bob. "In our room", he replied. "But we haven't got a room," I said.

It turned out that Whitesnake had booked us in and they picked up the bill. The mini-bar took quite a hiding as I was celebrating our great F.A. Cup result and confident of a good night ahead.

Then it was time to go. A limousine had been laid on to

take Bob and I to the gig and we were given real star treatment. We went straight to the bar where we met Dave Watson, the Manchester City and England defender, who was also a big fan of the group. After a couple of drinks we were taken to our seats, just seven rows from the stage. When the band came on the place erupted. They were wearing Middlesbrough shirts which I had given them and they gave me a mention before playing two and a half hours of unforgettable music. It was simply brilliant.

After the show we went backstage to congratulate the lads and then it was back to the hotel for a reception which had been laid on for the band. The first person I bumped into was snooker star Alex "Hurricane" Higgins. I had met him a few times previously when he had played in the Tolly Cobbold Snooker Classic in Ipswich and we had soon become friends. When the band arrived at the hotel Cozy Powell came straight to us and asked Alex if he had anything on him. We went to Alex's room where he took out this packet and then the penny dropped.

"Is that cocaine?" I asked.

"Yes, and it's bloody good stuff. Why not try some. It won't harm you," came back the reply.

After sniffing a little, I could not take anymore because I had broken my nose so many times I couldn't breathe properly. Alex and Cozy finished off the rest.

Alex then suggested we went back to his house for a game of snooker. He had the table he won the Embassy World Championship on in his games room, and after a while I started to feel a bit peculiar. I was assured I would soon get over it as Alex started to show us some trick shots. When we had another game I found I could not let go of the cue. It was as if someone had put my legs and arms in plaster and I couldn't move.

Cozy suggested that he had better take me back to the hotel. I can remember going to my room and feeling sick and then everything went blank. The next thing I remember was Bob picking me up off the bathroom floor.

I had been there all night, there was sick everywhere so Bob stuck me under the shower to clean me up before we headed back to Middlesbrough.

I slept all the way back and, before going to bed, told Bob

to wake me up in good time in the morning because I had to train. Come Monday morning and I felt no better and asked Bob to ring Malcolm Allison to say that I was ill. Later Malcolm came to see me and I told him the whole story and he was very sympathetic.

"Don't worry, Beat, we have all done it," said Malcolm. He told me not to report back until Wednesday, saying that I deserved a couple of extra days off. What a guy. As I said earlier, I just wished I could have played under him for a lot longer.

That was the first and last time I tried drugs. All I can say to anybody who takes them is don't. They will do you no good and in the case of footballers, will seriously damage your career.

18

Awards

Footballers who are successful throughout their careers are more often that not suitably rewarded. The higher level you play, obviously the rewards are greater, and I am not talking just about money.

It is always nice to be recognised for achievements and throughout my career I picked up some wonderful awards which I will treasure for the rest of my life. In many ways, as far as I was concerned, it all happened so quickly. I had made my first team debut for Ipswich Town at the start of the 1972-73 season against Manchester United at Old Trafford and by the end of that campaign I had picked up my first piece of silverware.

The Harwich branch of the Ipswich Town Supporters Club presented a rose bowl at the end of each season, and still do, for their player of the year and I won it in my first season. It was the highest honour any Town player could get and I'm told, with undue modesty, that I won it by a mile. Not many players have won it twice, but the very next season I was voted player of the year again, although it was much closer on that occasion. My career had hardly got off the ground, but I had already become a big favourite with the Ipswich supporters.

That season was unforgettable because I also received two other awards. The Professional Footballers Association have their own awards culminating with a big night at London's Hilton Hotel. It's a night when all the big names in football gather and when the P.F.A. Player of the Year and Young Player of the Year are announced.

It was the first time that I had been to an occasion like this. The Hilton was something else and as a young player rubbing shoulders with some of the great names was an experience to say the least.

I had no idea I was in line for the award. I assumed you had to be playing with one of the very big clubs to stand a chance, and I had gone to London with my team-mates for a night out. It was only when I got to the table where the Ipswich boys were sitting did I think that I had a chance of winning it. There was an X on my name place and I wondered if that meant something.

When my name was read out it took a few moments to digest and my legs literally turned to jelly as I walked from the table up to the stage to collect my award from Don Revie. He said, "I wish I could afford to have this kid in my team", and when it came to my turn to thank everybody that had voted for me, I felt tongue-tied, something that did not happen to me very often throughout my career. Anyway I said a few words and returned to my seat with the rest of the Ipswich players who were there slapping me on the back and shaking my hand.

Once I had got over what had been a complete shock, I was able to relax and things returned to normal. As it turned out I had one hell of a night. I cannot remember when I went upstairs to my bed, but I do have visions of dawn breaking over London!

In addition to winning the P.F.A. award I had also been selected in the First Division team of the year, something I achieved four years running. Just to round off a memorable season, I was also named as the Rothman's Young Player of the Year.

When Ipswich Town won the F.A. Cup in 1978 for the only time in their history, my home town of Carlisle decided to honour the achievement. Besides myself, two other players hailed from Carlisle, David Geddis, who set up the goal that defeated Arsenal, and Robin Turner, who was in the squad and had played in the team in several of the matches on the way to Wembley. David, Robin and I were given the Freedom of the City of Carlisle at a civic reception. That meant a great deal to me.

I've been lucky to have been given numerous awards throughout my career, but the one that really means the most to me was the one I received in 1993. The Ipswich Evening Star ran a competition for readers to select their greatest ever Ipswich Town player in the history of the club, and I came out on top and was presented with a solid gold watch. I had and still have a great rapport with the supporters in the town. Even today, I am still asked for my autograph although it can still have it's embarrassing moments.

Not so long ago I was invited to Portman Road for the launch of a video. Before the launch I was chatting to several of today's players out on the practice pitch which is behind the Pioneer Stand. There was a number of supporters present and they all wanted my autograph and a chat while they virtually ignored the other players. It's nice to be popular, but I wondered what the other players must have been thinking. At the time they were having a lean time and crowds were down. Perhaps I reminded them of the good old days.

It was also a fantastic honour to be invited to the twenty-fifth P.F.A. Dinner at the London Hilton in 1998. I was sitting on the top table with some great players, Peter Shilton, Dennis Bergkamp, and Pat Jennings. It was an absolutely superb night, and it was great to be interviewed by the television company covering the event and to give my story of being the first Young Player of the Year in 1973. It was great to see some old faces and some good mates, but it also made me think as to how I would have coped in the modern day game and the difference it may have made to my life.

19

Mr John

Mr John Cobbold was a one-off. When I first met him, I couldn't believe he was the chairman. Don't get me wrong, he was a wonderful fellow, but I'd always been led to believe that chairmen of football clubs were rarely seen, certainly not by the players. As far as I was concerned they were the figureheads of the football clubs, not people you could have a laugh and joke with and see on a regular basis.

Mr John, as he was known by everyone at Portman Road, simply didn't look like a chairman for a man in his position. His car, for instance, was an old Rover, driven by his chauffeur Roger, and had a television in the back. In the summer he always wore old khaki shorts and sandals with odd socks. He was definitely one of the boys. On away trips he always arranged for beer to be put on the bus. Although he was very wealthy, nothing was too much for him. He was different class.

There are many stories involving Mr John, but my favourite concerns a pre-season party at his home outside Ipswich at Glemham Hall. A week or so before each season, Mr John would lay on a party for all staff at the club, and I mean everybody. Nobody was forgotten. There was mountains of food and drink and the last words he used to say when everybody was there was "enjoy yourselves."

This particular night Mr John, Allan Hunter and myself wandered off for a cigarette. We got to the bottom of a field where there were three donkeys. Suddenly Mr John decided that each of us had to get on a donkey and have a race back to the house. He was so drunk that he fell off three or four times on the way, but he would not give up.

Local group, Barry Dye and the Sonics, were playing the music out on the patio as we approached on the donkeys. As we approached, Mr John shouted out: "How do you stop this bloody thing?" The next moment his donkey had jumped over a low fence and crashed straight into the drums which Barry was playing! Bobby Robson appeared wondering what was going on and, when he spotted me, obviously thought that I had been up to no good. Then he saw the chairman lying in a heap in the middle of the drums and the donkey nowhere to be seen.

Big Al quickly came to the rescue. He picked up Mr John, put him over his shoulder, and carried him off to bed. While this had all been going on, Paul Mariner had been up to his room and tied knots in his pyjamas. Half an hour later, with the party in full swing, Mr John came down the stairs wearing his pyjamas and looking like a scarecrow. Everybody fell about laughing. It was one of the funniest sights I have ever seen and it always sticks out in my mind.

A couple of days later Mr John came into the dressing room before training and said an incident like that is what this club is all about, and he treated everybody the same.

Mr John was no fool despite his pranks, and it is no coincidence that most of the best years at Portman Road were when he was chairman. Of course, there have been one or two well documented phrases, like the time when he asked if there was a crisis at the club and he replied: "The only time there is one is when the white wine runs out!".

I shall never forget the night that Mr John threw a party after the club had won the F.A. Youth Cup in 1973. It was a tremendous achievement to win the biggest youth competition in the country and Mr John made sure that it would be properly celebrated. All the parents of the boys from all over the country were invited at the chairman's expense and put up at the Copdock International Hotel. It was a lavish affair, but when Mr John got up to say a few words, he brought the house down.

He thanked the parents for coming from far and wide and finished with the never to be forgotten phrase: "Now go upstairs and produce another F.A. Youth Cup winning side!"

The Professional Footballers Associations' annual awards do at London's Hilton was one not to be missed. What a night that used to be, mingling with all the biggest names in the game, but as far as the Ipswich players were concerned, they had Mr John to thank for a wonderful night. He used to pay for all the

112

players to stay the night and before the dinner, gave a champagne reception in his suite. It was a lovely gesture by a terrific man.

When I played for England, players from other clubs would always ask about Mr John. His fame had spread and they were envious that at Ipswich we should have a chairman like him.

20

Some of the greats

When I look back over my career, I have been fortunate to play with and against some great players. I was lucky to play in some fine Ipswich Town sides under Bobby Robson and it's not unnatural that I have chosen the majority of the best players I have played with from that club, but when asked to name the players I had most difficulty playing against that was another matter.

To be honest, I found football, in the main, fairly easy and after a lot of soul searching, I could only name three. Let's have a look first at the best players I either played with or against. Best is appropriate because number one was definitely GEORGE BEST. He was a real superstar. I used to watch him when I was a kid. He wasn't tall or particularly strong, but it was a different matter trying to get the ball off him. In a nutshell he had everything and undoubtedly the greatest player I have ever seen. It was a pity that his career finished so early, but I reckon it was the English public and officialdom that drove him out of the game. They didn't give him enough space. There is no doubt he should have gone on a lot longer and I would certainly have liked to have played against him more times than I did.

BOBBY MOORE: I was lucky to be in two England squads at the same time as he was playing. I remember I used to call him "sir". He was such a nice man and a real gent. He wasn't big headed, just one of the boys. I remember when I was called into the senior squad for the first time. I had been picked for the Under-23 squad to play in Italy. We were in the airport departure lounge when Sir Alf Ramsey told me and Mike Pejic that we had been switched to the full squad. Almost immediately Bobby came across and welcomed Mike and I and made us feel at home. As far as I was concerned, he was God.

COLIN BELL: What a superb and sometimes underrated

player he was. He had the nickname, "Nijinski", which was appropriate because I have never seen a player run as much as he did during a game. He knew exactly where to run and when he was on the ball he was always in control. He was the greatest midfielder, and not far behind George Best. There were no airs or graces about Colin and he made everybody around him so relaxed. He certainly didn't get the recognition he deserved, but for my money he was one of the world's best.

BOBBY CHARLTON: Although I only played against him a couple of times, I feel I was so lucky to have been in opposition to somebody of his calibre. What he did with the ball was different class. He never got himself into trouble and always knew what he would do with the ball, and two good feet helped him as well. I always thought that John Wark had studied Bobby a great deal when he was starting his career and certain things, like the way he broke from midfield, obviously rubbed off on Warky.

ALAN BALL: I played in the same England team as him, but I would have given anything to have played in the same club side week in, week out. Bally was a great motivator, had a heart as big as an elephant and was as strong as an ox. On top of that he was a real winner. I wished he had played for Ipswich.

Now to the Ipswich players and top of my list is ALLAN HUNTER, which won't come as any great surprise. He was simply tremendous as I have pointed out in an earlier chapter. Whenever I was on international duty, either with the full squad or the Under-23's, his name invariably cropped up in conversation. I never found one player who liked to play against him, and that included all the top names in the game.

MICK MILLS: A tremendous captain and a superb leader. It didn't matter at Portman Road whether you were an international or a kid that had just come into the team, he treated everybody the same. Mick was a big influence on my game. He often used to sit down and talk to me about the game in general and pick up on any points he felt would be to my advantage. He knows so much about football and I reckon he would have made a good England manager. I've got so much respect for him.

ARNOLD MUHREN and FRANS THIJSSEN: You cannot

115

say enough about these two. They were two of the greatest midfield players I have ever seen. What a great coup it was when Bobby Robson brought the two Dutchmen to Portman Road. Certainly they will never be forgotten. Both had so much composure, yet they were different in many ways. I remember in their early days at Ipswich everybody wanted to be on their side in the five-a-sides. The team with Arnold and Sam McLeod, as Frans was known, always won so the gaffer had to change it and made sure they were on opposite sides.

Frans was the all-round player. I remember Mick Mills christening him Captain Hook for the way he used to keep control of the ball by wrapping his leg around it like a hook and making it very difficult for the opposition to take it off him.

Arnold was a superb player although maybe he wasn't tough enough and wasn't a great header of the ball, but his left foot was superb. He could drop the ball on a shilling from fifty yards and the service he provided down the channels was the making of Alan Brazil.

TREVOR WHYMARK: The best header of a ball I've ever seen. As a target man he was brilliant. Nine times out of ten he would win the ball in the air, but he didn't get the praise he deserved. To my mind, Trevor was different class when it came to heading, but he could also play on the deck. It was scandalous to think he was only capped once by England.

A few years ago when the readers of the Ipswich Evening Star selected their greatest all time Ipswich Town team, what surprised me was that Trevor was edged out by Ray Crawford. I never saw Ray play, but all I can say is that he must have been one hell of a player to have beaten Trevor in the poll.

PAUL MARINER: A real character was PM, but he was hungry for his football. He was a big, strong guy who was aggressive even in practice matches. I didn't enjoy marking him when I played against him which I invariably did because the first team defence played against the midfield players and strikers. I always reckoned he was a leader from the front and my one regret is that I didn't get the chance to play in the same England team with him, apart from a brief substitute's appearance against Luxembourg. Never short of a word, PM was always the first to encourage you especially if you were having a bad game, and invariably he would help get you back playing your normal game.

GEORGE BURLEY: What a good player he was, especially quick as there was nothing of him, but he was strong, and could run all day. Considering his physique he was not easy to knock off the ball. When we had a back four at Ipswich of George, Big Al, myself and Millsy, that was the best in the land, no doubt about it.

What sticks in my mind is that he was always a good listener. When Bobby Robson was speaking he never missed a word and I am not surprised that he gone on to become a manager.

Last, but certainly not least, is JOHN WARK: His record speaks for itself. I've never seen anybody read the game as he did and his ability to find space between defenders was uncanny. Remember he started and finished his career at the back, but it was as a midfield player where he really made his name and his goal scoring record from that department has been as good as anybody in the game. It was a tremendous feat when he equalled Jose Altafini's goal scoring record in the year Ipswich won the UEFA Cup in 1981, although that has now been beaten by Jürgen Klinsmann. Warky had all-round ability and I cannot praise his contribution to Ipswich Town enough.

Now we come to the three players I least liked playing against.

ANDY GRAY: I used to hate marking him. He was awkward and never gave you a minute's peace. One thing was certain, you knew you had been in a game. He was a tough player and would run through a brick wall if asked to and certainly was the hardest player I played against. When he was at Aston Villa he was particularly effective in his partnership with Peter Withe. One thing is certain, I always came off at the end with bumps and bruises after facing Andy.

KEVIN KEEGAN: Big defenders like me always favoured marking players of similar size, so when you came up against someone of Kevin's stature and ability it always caused more problems. The best way I can describe him is that he was like a little terrier snapping at your heels. Even though he was small, he was good in the air and you never knew what he was going to do next. If you got too close to him, he was liable to leave you with egg on your face by turning past you, so I tended to step back a yard, but even that did not guarantee success.

STEVE KINDON: For a big man, he had so much pace and was one of the quickest players I ever faced. He was hard to knock off the ball, and if he got a yard ahead of me, I could never catch him, and I was renowned for my speed!

I also thought I had to write something about today's so called HARDMEN, i.e, Vinny Jones, David Batty, Paul Ince, Neil "Razor" Ruddock. Well, I played with and against men who make them look like pussy-cats. The guys I am about to talk about would eat them alive.

The first one is my old sparring partner Allan Hunter. You could kick him around all day and he would come back for more and off the pitch he was the same. When we went out for a drink he would take no shit off anyone. There have been a few times when we have been confronted by guys with a load of beer in them trying to get him going but the big man always said, "I will give you a chance, go and sober up then come back." As you can guess his offer was never taken up. Good job as he would have made mincemeat out of them.

Then there was Tommy Smith. He had muscles on his muscles. When we played Liverpool I always noticed our winger, Clive Woods, never played well against him. I found out the reason why. I was coming back to the dressing room after inspecting the pitch for what studs to put in for the game and there was Tommy talking to Woodsy, who was as white as a ghost. Tommy just nodded at me and said, "O.K. Beat, looking forward to meeting you, if you go on one of your runs up front."

"Great," I said, "can't wait."

I spoke to Woodsy and he said big Tommy just threatened to put me in hospital. Well to cut a long story short, Clive played on the right wing instead of the left and kept well away from Tommy. I had a good old ding-dong but after the game we had a laugh and a joke.

What do you think of this for a "Hardman" team. I bet that no player of the past or of the present would like to play against them.

In goal it has to be Big Joe Corrigan. This man was a giant. Solid as a rock and when Big Joe came out for crosses you did not want to be in his way. I have, and I thought an oak tree had hit me.

Right-back. Tommy Smith, he would tackle a bull.

In the middle of my back four would be Kenny Burns and Norman Hunter. Both were as hard as nails and they would run through a brick wall. Jimmy Case once wrote about me as being the complete player, the complete hard man, football's Daley Thompson. So I have to put myself at left-back even though I did not like playing in that position.

So to the midfield. Graeme Souness, he had skill to match his fierce tackling and his love of the game.

Archie Gemmill, not a big man but he was so tough he never shirked a challenge.

Nobby Stiles, another small man with a big heart. He took no prisoners, a player who would kick you and say don't worry Beat we will have a drink afterwards and compare bruises.

Now the front three. Andy Gray, I have already talked about him but he would head heads, the post, the stand and still get up and smile.

Mark Hughes, he is still playing and putting himself about. Very strong, very hard to knock off the ball.

Fianlly, Joe Jordan. When he played with his teeth out he looked even more frightening and would kick anything that he saw, even his own teammates. He was very quiet off the field though.

Well, you so called "hard men", you would have had no chance against this team and that is a promise.

21

Playing abroad

It was a bitter blow when I was told my career was over. I felt that I had a few more years left in me, but the pain I had been through and the countless injections had finally taken their toll. However, it was not the end as far as playing football at some level was concerned. It was a question of taking things a bit easier and playing at a lower level where there would not be the same pressure on my knee.

After a complete break, I eased my way back slowly. Several people approached me with the view to helping out and finally I decided to take the plunge with Ipswich United in the local Suffolk and Ipswich League.

The late Jimmy Barker was the man behind United. He was a larger than life character whom I had known for several years. Jimmy often came on the trips with the official Town party when we were playing in Europe and I remember him once saying to me that if I wanted a game when I had finished my career he would be please to accommodate me at United.

I also knew several of their players at that time and it was a case of me easing my way back without the pressures. I played several games for United before I received an offer from Tony Armstrong who was the manager of Jewson League side Harwich and Parkeston.

That was a step up, but it was something I was able to handle and I played for a season at the Royal Oak. Those were thoroughly enjoyable times, but now I felt I needed something more permanent and it was a case of earning some money.

I had remained in touch with Ron Gray who had been chief scout at Portman Road for several years. Ron had been in the game a long time and had contacts all over the place. One day he rang me to sat that he had fixed me up with a club in Sweden. It was a good offer and Maggie and I decided to take

(above): I was the first Ipswich player to receive a sponsored car. Here I am with the Ford Cortina with Terry Robinson and Frank Howard. What about the hair styles and tank top? (below): John and Graeme Keeble, without them I would have had no way of getting about for the past year. Many thanks for all your help. P.S. The Jag is for sale.

It is my wedding day, so time to look extra smart.
This is me with my best man, Steven Strawn.
What about the Vampire Bats around our necks?

A bad hair day at Tottenham for me and Spurs' Chris McGrath.

When the "gaffer" said get it upfield, he meant it. Here on a wet night at Tottenham I prevent Chris Jones from getting anywhere near the ball.

(left): Clive Woods may be quick, but he will never overtake me now.

(opposite page): (top) Brian Talbot and David Johnson carry me shoulder high as I parade my PFA Young Player of the Year Award in 1973.

(bottom): Twenty-five years on and here I am with Denis Bergkamp, Gordon Taylor and David Platt at the 1998 PFA Player of the Year Award Ceremony. We only need a keeper for a very good five-a-side team.

Some of the greats: Mick Mills. P.S. He's the one on the chair!!

(below):
Some of
the greats:
Sir Bobby
Charlton.

(above):
Some of the greats: John Wark.

(above):
Some of the greats: Kevin Keegan,
who said Alan Shearer was his most famous signing??

(left):
Some of
the greats:
Steve Kindon, an
unsung star, he
was one of the
quickest players I
played against. I
certainly would
have needed that
police motorbike
to catch him.

Some of the greats: Colin "Nijinski" Bell.

Some of the greats: Bobby Moore, to me he was God.

Some of the greats: Andy Gray, he went on to prove that
the Sky is the limit, but a real hard man on the pitch.

Some of the greats: George Burley

(above):
Some of the greats: Frans Thijssen and Arnold Muhren.
Everybody wanted to be in their five-a-side team.
(below):
Some of the greats: Trevor Whymark, a brilliant header of the
ball but here seen shooting against Leeds United.

Some of the greats: Alan Ball, he has a heart as big as an
elephant and was as strong as an ox. He was also a great
leader and I would have loved to have played
alongside him at club level.

Me and three of my greatest fans, my daughters pictured
above in 1979, and below in Middlesbrough in 1982.
Me and my "hat-trick".

The best team I have ever had.
(standing): Sarah, Louise, Emma (daughters).
(seating on the arms of the chair): Hannah, myself with Josh.
(seating in the chair): Maggie (my wife) with Keiron.

(left)
Another one from
my wedding day,
but this time with
the lady with
whom I have
shared most of
my life, Maggie.

the plunge. The club was Sandviking that played in the Second Division and things worked out very well. I started off playing up front but ended up as a sweeper. My knee stood up because it was so much easier playing. I was able to rest after matches, yet I was still able to train. I remember when the winter came, we used to train in the snow, wearing rubber moulded boots with spikes in them!

In my second season I was voted Player of the Year, the first time a foreigner had achieved this, but we didn't have a strong enough squad to win promotion. At the end of that season the coach got the sack and the new man didn't want foreigners in the team. It was a bitter disappointment. Sweden was a lovely country, even though it was very cold in the winter, and I had enjoyed my one year but there was nothing else I could do, so back to Ipswich we came and I rejoined Harwich.

Then one day I received a letter from Bryan King, the former Millwall, Coventry City and England Under-23 goalkeeper, who had also had a spell at Portman Road as the specialised goalkeeping coach. Being based in Scandinavia, Bryan had heard of my plight. He was the boss at Kongsberg who played in Division Four in Norway. It was the club where Danny Olsen, later to have a spell at Portman Road, had started his career and Bryan reckoned I could do a good job for him.

I decided that it would be a good move, even at that level, and in my first season I played up front and scored sixty goals, which helped gain the club promotion.

Christmas 1987 was a time of my life that I'll never forget, but for all the wrong reasons. It had started out innocently enough, coming back to England from Norway to do some Christmas shopping, but ended up in a police cell, arrested for being overdue on a library book which wasn't even mine!

It was Saturday, December 10th when I arrived at Harwich after a voyage from Oslo via Denmark. The thirty-six hour journey had been rough, but I was happy enough when I saw my mate Barry waiting for me on the quayside to take me to Ipswich. I had decided to come home to do the Christmas shopping because it was much cheaper than it was in Norway. In any case it was nice to have a few days back home to catch up with old friends, have a few drinks and a natter in the Belsted

Arms and pop round to see the in-laws.

Then it was time to do the shopping, something I have always hated, but it had to be done. Maggie had given me a list as long as your arm as to what to get for the girls and after three days of traipsing around the streets and shops of Ipswich, I had brought everything.

After a few nights out, it was time to return to Norway in time for Christmas. Barrys' son Wayne and his wife Gail gave me a lift to Harwich to catch the last boat before the festive season. That was when everything started to go wrong. I was weighed down with so many bags full of presents that it took me three trips to get through passport control. I was just preparing to make my third trip when I noticed three blokes going through my other bags. When I challenged them, demanding what they were doing, they told me they were customs men. I was taken to a nearby room when the biggest of the three said that they were not, in fact, customs, but the police. They told me that I was under arrest and I would be told what for once I had been taken to Ipswich Police Station. I told them that this was the last ship going to Norway before Christmas and that I had better be on it.

That cut no ice whatsoever and I was bundled into a car and taken to Harwich Police Station. I was told there would be a van coming from Ipswich to pick me up.

After half an hour they decided to take me to Ipswich themselves, me in one car and my presents in another. On arrival I had my finger-prints taken and then had to wait what seemed ages before, of all people, my old team-mate from Portman Road, John Peddelty, walked into the cell.

John was now a policeman and when I asked him what the charge was, he told me I was overdue with the payment on a library book. I told him I didn't even belong to a library, and I'm sure he believed me. There was £7 to pay and as I had over £800 in my wallet, I told John to take the money out of that.

After checking with his superiors, John told me I was free to go. I was not a very happy man. I phoned my mate Barry and told him where I was. He came and picked me up and took me back to his house. The ship,of course, had long since sailed. I phoned Maggie to tell her what had happened and then I had to try and get a flight to be back in Norway by Christmas Day. I managed to book a flight on Christmas Eve, but had to pay for two seats after explaining the amount of luggage I had with me. Anyway, all seemed well as I eventually got going for a second time.

Going through the x-ray machine at the airport, the guy in charge suddenly burst out laughing. I had forgotten I had bought a large chicken and put it in my hand luggage and on the x-ray machine all that showed up was the skeleton!

To be honest, I hate flying and always have done, but on this occasion it was a necessity. After flying to Oslo to be greeted by three feet of snow on the ground, there was still a ninety minute drive ahead to Kongberg. When I finally arrived home I was out on my feet after the hassle of the previous couple of days. The girls were in bed before Maggie told me the truth about the library book.

She had taken it out of the library the last time I was in England and she had signed the card in my name. I didn't know what to say, but being Christmas I forgave her.

Everything was rosy but before the start of the following season Bryan was sacked and the Kongsberg chairman offered me the job as player-coach, but he was out-voted by his board of directors who did not want an Englishman holding that post.

Within days there was interest from Nybersund, who played in the Second Division. They impressed me when I spoke to them and I decided to sign. Nybersund was a ski resort and I have never seen so much snow in all my life. I spent two seasons there and I remember that Maggie and I had to dig ourselves out of our chalet on several occasions!

As far as the football was concerned, Nybersund didn't have a big enough squad and as a result never had a realistic chance of winning anything. Again, it was an experience and certainly playing did not come hard to me.

After two years I moved on, this time to Frederikstad where I was told I would be able to find a job, but the best that was on offer was playing Division Five or Six and I didn't fancy that. So I did a bit of coaching but by now I was beginning to feel homesick.

It was soon after we were back that Maggie noticed an

139

advertisement in the Evening Star for a bar manager at the Cross Keys at Henley, a village on the outskirts of Ipswich.

It was now 1989, but I landed the job and stayed there for just over a year before taking up a similar appointment at The Waveney in Bramford Road, which is now known as Churchills.

I also returned to football briefly, playing a couple of games for Clacton in the Jewson League, and I even managed them for a while. Even though I had been out of the country for some time, I found I was still in demand. I turned out in numerous charity matches, before the bottom dropped out of my world.

22

Home Town Dream

It's every footballer's dream to play for their home town club, and I am no exception. I was born and bred in Carlisle, but apart from playing against them once when I was an Ipswich player, that was that.

When I was a boy I used to go to Brunton Park, but as the club in those days did not have a youth system there was little chance of me playing for them. Unfortunately, Carlisle United have only been in the top flight for one season and that was in 1974, but when they came to Portman Road in November they were top of the First Division table. We defeated them 3-1 and it was a wonderful feeling because many of my old school mates came to Suffolk for the game. I met them afterwards and they told me it would be a different story when Ipswich went to Carlisle later in the season.

The lads all wanted to bet on the outcome, so I had a £5 bet with the lot of them. It was in February that we we played the return league fixture.

We were booked in at the Hill Top Hotel, which was about half a mile from my parents house. After dinner I asked Bobby Robson if it would be all right to go and see my family. Robson said it would be fine as long as I kept out of the Magpie pub!

I said, "Don't you trust me? This is one of the most important games of the season for me, so you don't have to worry."

When I got to my parents house all the family were there – aunts, uncles, brothers, sisters, cousins, the lot. After a natter and taking a fair bit of stick, I went down to the pub where my dad was playing dominoes. When he saw me, he said: "Lend me a fiver son. I'm on a roll." I gave him the fiver, had an orange juice and a chat with the lads.

Then I went back to the hotel and found Robson waiting in

the reception. After asking if everybody was well, he told me that I was going to captain the side against my home town club. What an honour.

Following breakfast on the day of the match we had a team meeting. Robson had the habit of repeating himself, so by the time he had finished we had forgotten what he had said in the first place. Then it was time to hand out the tickets. None of the other players wanted theirs, so the boss gave me the lot. I needed them to cater for my family.

When we arrived at the ground all the family were waiting. I gave them their tickets and told them I'd see them in the bar afterwards. As to the game itself, we started badly and were soon a goal down before Trevor Whymark equalised. We got a right roasting from Robson at half-time and we deserved it.

Early in the second half Carlisle scored again, but despite being on top we could not score a second. I was convinced that I was going to score following a corner when I rose above everyone and headed the ball towards the top corner of the goal, but somehow the Carlisle goalkeeper managed to get his fingertips to it and turn it behind for another corner. From that one I again won a header, but was inches off target.

The final whistle went and we had lost 2-1. The Carlisle fans poured on to the pitch and congratulated me on missing two headers!

Anyway, I stayed in Carlisle for the weekend and was treated like a king. Unfortunately United were relegated at the end of the season. They were just not strong enough.

To this day, people in Carlisle still talk about that match and I keep telling them that if their goalkeeper had not made that great save from my header, they would have gone down earlier!

23

Fun and on the run

Playing for your country is one of the biggest honours in the game and I only wished I could have won more caps. One thing was for sure, when I was with the international squad there was a great deal of micky-taking, and the biggest joker of them all was the Manchester United winger, Gordon Hill.

On one occasion the squad had been given the day off by manager, Don Revie, so it was arranged for the team to visit the Brent Cross Shopping Centre in North London. Gordon had other ideas and asked me whether I fancied going on a tour of London. That had more appeal, so off we went. "Hilly" had decided on Soho, and what amazed me was that he seemed to know everyone there. He took me into a joke shop where we each bought a mask. They were gruesome to say the least.

Then he said we would go to the pictures to see Black Emmanuel and wind up some of the punters, especially the old blokes, that would be there. No sooner had we sat down than "Hilly" had disappeared. I wondered where he had gone when all of a sudden there was a scream at the front and a number of old blokes came running up the aisle, all with long coats on and trying to cover themselves up. They were obviously flashers. With his mask on, "Hilly" had scared the life out of them. The cinema manager was not pleased, so we made a hasty exit.

When we got back to the hotel, we sneaked up to the room being shared by the Liverpool pairing of Ray Clemence and Ian Callaghan. After knocking a couple of times and hearing a voice say, "come in", we did nothing because we wanted one of them to answer the door. Eventually there was a response. Ray opened the door but he must have shot back at least twenty feet when he saw these two figures with ugly masks on. What a laugh. We did it to everybody in the squad with the same routine, but when we got to Joe Corrigan's room he kept shouting that he was on the phone. Well we rushed into his room and told him that it would improve his features if he wore one of the masks. He dropped the phone and gave chase, but fortunately we had a head start. Big Joe was not a person to wind up.

Later that evening "Hilly" and I ordered tea and sandwiches from room service. When the lad brought them up we went to our door with sheets and masks on. He nearly had a fit. He dropped the tray while we were laughing our heads off, but we helped him clean up and gave him a big tip.

Les Cocker, Revie's second in command, used to have a row in a boat every morning on a pond in the grounds of the hotel. One morning "Hilly" and I rigged the boat so it would sink. We attached a rope to the plug in the boat and then hid behind a bush to wait for Les. When he reached the middle of the pond we pulled out the cork and the boat sank. Les was screaming that he couldn't swim, and as there was nobody about, "Hilly" and I decided we had better go to the rescue. We dived in and there was a big thud as we hit the bottom and when we stood up the water only came up to our knees! Les was laughing his head off and the rest of the squad were hanging out of their bedroom windows, shouting and applauding.

What we did not know was that Les had overheard our plan to scupper the boat and decided to tell the boys what was going to happen. "Hilly" and I thought we were going to have a big laugh, but it was Les and the boys who definitely had the bigger one.

On another England squad gathering we went to the London Palladium to see a show called The Comedians which starred Tommy Cooper and Bernard Manning. Tommy announced that the England football squad was in the audience and asked everyone to give us a round of applause. It was a proud moment. Then Tommy wanted someone out of the audience to help with a trick. He pointed to Kevin Keegan. Tommy asked him if he had a watch and Kevin showed him his Rolex. He asked Kevin if he could borrow his watch and then wrapped it in a handkerchief before hitting it with a hammer. When he opened the hankie the watch was a real mess and looking at Kevin's face I thought he was going to cry. Tommy said he was sorry, and told him that normally the trick worked before taking him back to his seat.

At the end of the show we were invited back stage for a drink, soft ones only insisted the gaffer, and something to eat. Tommy asked Kevin if he wanted something to eat, but said he would prefer to have his watch back. Eventually Kevin said he would have a roll and when he bit into it, the rest of us were expecting that he would find his watch. But no, it was just a cheese and onion roll.

The answer to Kevin's "smashed" watch was soon revealed when Tommy told him he had slipped it back into his pocket as the left the stage. It had proved a great laugh and Kevin was a very relieved man.

They were great times and I miss them very much. I wonder if today's players have such a good time?

I was invited as a representative of Ipswich Town Football Club with other players to compete in a special 100 yard sprint which the Professional Footballers Association had arranged in Gateshead in the mid-seventies. I was chosen by the club as Bobby Robson and Cyril Lea had once clocked me at running 100 yards on grass in football boots at 10 seconds dead. They thought I was a sure bet to win the 100 yards sprint. The idea was to find out who was the fastest sprinter in professional football.

It is quite a drive from Ipswich for the Gateshead run, and Charlie Woods being a Geordie knew the best route. Charlie was the youth team/reserve team manager when I was at the football club, and only recently Charlie left Ipswich to join Tottenham Hotspur as chief scout. We stopped off at Charlie's in-laws for a cuppa and a sandwich. Charlie's in-laws are great people and made me very welcome. They asked if it was worth a bet on me winning. "Yes", I said, "I stand a good chance".

We got to the stadium and there were people everywhere, as I did not realise this was also an athletics meeting. I spotted Dave Moorcroft, whom I had met in Ipswich when we presented the Round the Town race trophies, and we went over for a chat. What a great chap, so down to earth.

I also had a natter with Brendon Foster who said, "please

will you sign for Newcastle United?". I was running against Malcolm Macdonald, Alan Kennedy and three other lads. Supermac was favourite. He was full of it, and he also had his own starting blocks to gain an advantage.

The starter lined us up and off went the gun. I got a good start with Supermac and Alan Kennedy. We were yards in front of the others. It was very close at half way and I was confident because the second fifty yards were normally my best. I got up speed and then powered on. Then all of a sudden I had to stop, my "twig and berries", as Charlie called them, came out of my shorts. What had happened was because I never wore a jock strap and the shorts I was wearing were to small for me they came out. Well I put everything together and started again, I was catching them up but the line came too soon. I was beaten on the dip. Supermac and Alan beat me but a few yards more and who knows? Well I know, I would have won. I looked round and Charlie was rolling on the ground with laughter.

We had to go and get our trophies and when I went for mine the crowd gave me the biggest cheer of the day. Dave Moorcroft said I should have left everything hanging as I might have won by a short d**k.

Every time I see Charlie he still reminds me to wear a jock strap and we have a good laugh about it.

Back in the 1970's there were not a great deal of agents on the scene. I used to go to England get togethers and ear-hole all the other lads as they talked about getting agents and I thought to myself that I should get into that.

Well, I had the chance. I was playing against Spurs one Saturday afternoon at White Hart Lane and after the game I was approached by this chap. He introduced himself as Julian Ascombe, and he told me that he had just started up his own agency.

I invited him into the players lounge and we got talking. He had all the credentials, letters, a big cigar, all the "schpeel". We arranged to meet the following week after an Ipswich Town home match. We met in the players lounge and he had a suit on that Liberace would have been proud to own.

He started to tell me all about his businesses and other

matters and he really impressed Maggie and I.

"O.K." I said, "let's have a months trial."

The following week he invited Maggie and myself down to London. After a great lunch in a posh restaurant he took us to Madame Tussauds. I was very impressed until he asked us to go back to his home for some tea.

We got back to this council house and he tried to explain that he was moving and staying with a mate.

"O.K, no bother," I said.

The week after that he had got me a big contract with a shampoo firm. No cash, but plenty of shampoo, he even supplied Ipswich Town Football Club. So every time, after training, the lads were using the best shampoo and not scrounging off everyone else.

I had begun to think there was something peculiar about this chap. He acted, well if I say, feminine, it would be an under-statement, but no-one said anything about it, even the lads were smitten. I remember Maggie saying to me that there was something false about this chap, but I took no notice, a woman's intuition, I guess.

That year it was Colin Harper's Testimonial and he had a golf match arranged. Trevor Whymark and I were to meet up with the England Under-23 squad on the evening of the golf day, so we played for Colin.

It was pissing down. I can't play golf so I had had a bad day and was dripping wet and very cold. After the round two big guys approached me and got a photograph out and they asked if I knew this person.

"Yes," I said, "he is my trial agent."

The photograph had this guy in a wig and a dress. I nearly fell over. The chaps were policemen and they told me that he was a con-man as well as being a transvestite. I went ape-shit and wanted to kill this "thing". They explained he had been going around football clubs doing to players what he had done to me.

That put me off agents for life. Mind you, I got, and the club got, loads of shampoo for nothing. I had never paid as much as a penny to him but when I think now what could have happened it makes me shudder. So be careful you young players. By the way my arse is still in one piece but if I saw the twat now, I would rip his balls off. Mind you, he might just enjoy that!

24

At death's door and now...

It was just a normal day at the pub as far as I was concerned, and little did I know I could have been dead twenty-four hours later,

Sunday was always a busy day, but no more than usual that day back in 1991. It was in the evening when my troubles really started. I got some cramps in my stomach, but I didn't think too much about them until they started to become worse. I went upstairs to have a lie on the bed, hoping they would go away, but ended up collapsing on the floor in agony. By then, of course, I knew there could be something very wrong.

Maggie phoned for the doctor late Sunday night, but it was not until first thing Monday morning that he was able to come and see me. By now the pain was excruciating. I had a terrible night wondering what was wrong with me. Had I been overdoing things was the first thought that went through my mind. Was it down to life running a pub, the long hours and the temptation to drink more than usual?

When the doctor arrived, he took one look at me and called for an ambulance. Besides the pain, worry started to set in. There must be something serious to get me into hospital in such a rush.

I was taken straight to a ward, but I could not get into bed properly. I was kneeling on the bed because I was simply unable to straighten up. I was given some painkillers, and they certainly helped and then I was told that appendicitis was suspected.

After a week in hospital I was sent home, but I couldn't eat or drink. Maggie phoned for the doctor again and told him that if I wasn't taken back into hospital immediately, she would take me there herself. By now I had lost a great deal of weight because I was only able to suck an ice cube. At the hospital they still couldn't find out what was wrong with me. By a big stroke of luck, one of the doctors at the hospital was a Dr Cameron who happened to be a big Town supporter and he had heard about my plight. He suggested I should have what is called a cat scan and it soon revealed that I had pancreas trouble.

Having established what I was suffering from was fine, but there was worse to come. Maggie was told that the success rate of an operation wasn't very high. It was decided, however, to open me up to confirm that I was suffering from an infection of the pancreas, but then they sewed me up. Had they touched the pancreas region I would have died on the operating table.

By now my weight had gone down from sixteen stones to nine stones and I looked like a withered old man. I had to be fed through a tube and there were drips on most parts of my body. My skin was a horrible grey colour and that really frightened Maggie. I am told I literally looked like death.

There was nothing I could do. I just lay on the bed for days on end, not seeming to get any better.

These were tough times for Maggie. She had a family to look after as well as worrying about me. Not being able to drive didn't help, so every night she used to phone the hospital to see how I was. There was no change for several days, until one night she phoned to be told that I wasn't too good.

Maggie immediately came to the hospital and I remember we tried to watch a film on the television. I couldn't really concentrate on anything and then it was decided I should be put into intensive care.

The outlook was really looking bleak. By now I could not stop shaking and my teeth were chattering, yet, of course, it was warm in the hospital. I had a secondary injection through the drips and was so pumped full of morphine that I felt like a drug addict, but at last I started to get better to such an extent that I was allowed to have visitors.

It was diagnosed that I had pancreatis, something I had never heard of, but because I was such a fit fellow I survived.

It transpired that my body had gone toxic through infection and it was that that nearly killed me. Maggie had become a diabetic through worry. They had been trying times indeed.

By the time I came out of hospital I had been there fourteen weeks and it's certainly something I would never want to go through again.

A couple of months later I had a relapse and was taken straight back to hospital, but after a week I was home again. There had been no change to my condition, but the hospital authorities were not taking any chances.

The trouble had all started through drinking and then not eating, perhaps the penalty of being a publican. I had to pack the job in and ever since I have been more careful with my diet and intake.

It certainly taught me a lesson, but in many ways I suppose I have to be grateful for small mercies. At one stage in those darkest days I was given just four hours to live, but my strength and fitness from my playing days seemed to pull me through.

It is a burden I have had to bear ever since. My illness, coupled with escape from death certainly changed me, and more recently a further scare when I was rushed into hospital in early 1998 with a suspected stroke has also changed me.

I did not drink a drop of alcohol for a couple of years after the pancreatis and started to think of my family much more. When my three daughters, Emma, Sarah and Louise were growing up I didn't really see much of them as I was away so much with my football. In the past few years I have got to know my children and my grandchildren much better. I became a grandfather at the ripe old age of 37 when Emma gave birth to Hannah. Since then she had had Josh and my youngest daughter, Louise, has also had a little boy, Kieran, who was born on March 1st 1997.

The grandchildren certainly take up a great deal of my time which I am delighted about because I have been unable to work since I came out of hospital. The pancreatis left me very weak and it had taken me a long time to get back my strength and I also have a bad back in the shape of a disc problem which stems from my playing days. To be honest, I struggle to walk on certain days. I was told by a specialist years ago that when I reached my forties, I would encounter problems.

The right side of my back, right knee and right calf seem to

151

seize up if I try and do too much. In fact I cannot walk more than a couple of hundred yards without feeling pain and having to stop and give them time to settle down. I bet I am not the only ex-footballer who struggles. O.K, it is great to be fit and healthy when you are young, but when you have to suffer when you finish, no-one tells you about that side of football. Mind you, I would still do the same if I had the chance all over again.

However, I would definitely see the proper people if I was injured and even though I gave up playing professional and non-league football some years ago, I did try and turn out in charity games whenever I could. The problem is the fact that I receive benefit now and I have just read in one newspaper that Tommy Smith, the ex-Liverpool hard man, lost all his benefit money because he took a penalty that was televised and somebody from the D.S.S. saw him and reported him.

O.K, Tommy got benefit for being disabled. Surely these people know what goes on and that he only took two steps and hit the ball. He did not run in the London Marathon. I bet the person was an Evertonian!

I cannot play in charity games now because of the situation and life is a bit of a struggle, but I know there are many people worse off than me. I receive the D.S.S. money and get the rent paid on my house. I have a little pension every month which provides me and my family with an income. We have not had a holiday for many years but it is something I try not to think about. My burning ambition is to take the whole family to Disneyland in Florida because I went there with Ipswich Town and I was like a kid again. So I would love to see my grand-childrens' faces when or if we get there. Certainly it is hard to envisage at the present time, but you never know. I have a couple of pounds on the National Lottery every week and I will keep my fingers crossed.

What I do know is that my problems now seem small in comparison to Maggie's. When I was in hospital with pancreatis, Maggie became a diabetic and ever since has to inject herself twice a day with insulin.

In 1996 a real bombshell dropped on our doorstep when it was discovered Maggie had contracted Multiple Sclerosis. She had not been well for over a year, but never in our wildest dreams did we think she had anything so serious. It's not fair, she would not harm a fly. She would give away her last penny to the poor, but after a scan it was confirmed she had M.S. We were devastated. We have asked ourselves many times, what has she done to deserve this?

That news put me down even more and the doctor reckoned she had contracted M.S. fourteen months earlier, but said they had found out just in time. Maggie still has regular treatment, but it never gets her down. She is a real star and she carries on with life just the same. She feels there is no point in sitting around thinking about it. I hope that one day a cure is found for M.S. because I would do anything for Maggie to be at the front of the queue to have the treatment.

I am looking forward to my grandsons growing up because I would love one of them to play football and put on the blue and white shirt of Ipswich and you never know, maybe the white of England.

I was doing a bit of scouting for Norwich City recently, thanks to Mike Walker and Duncan Forbes. You might well think, why Norwich? Well no-one else asked me. I would love to get back into the great game somehow as I think that with my knowledge of defending I surely must be able to help some club in the future. I would also like to think I have a good eye for players as I watch a lot of non-league games. I think there are a lot of good players out there and I do try to help them in getting trials for local league clubs. The only problem is a lot of clubs want players to go straight into the first team, but do not realise the lads need to train and be involved in professional football before they can play.

I an now doing a bit of scouting for my old mate Alan Ball at Portsmouth which I am enjoying immensely. I recently watched Norwich City play Queen's Park Rangers for Pompey with my mate Mark Lomas, who is also my agent. After the game we were diverted by a local Norwich bobby through a one way system in the town. As we were driving along I pointed out to Mark that I used to work for BB Brickwork, in 1996, doing a bit of labouring to get fit, and built a signal box about two hundred yards from the Norwich City football ground. The owner of the Company, Brian Bloomfield (Bloomie) used to really wind up the Norwich supporters who walked along by pointing me out saying; "Did they recognise the guy who was now mixing cement and carrying bricks into the building?".

I had a lot of fun working for Bloomie and drinking in the local pubs with the Norwich supporters. It is a real small world because I was recently at a sportsman's dinner where George Best was a speaker and I bumped into Bloomie, who I hadn't seen for a while. I told him that I would recommend some local brickies to him and I am sure he would look after them. By the way, the George Best night was brilliant and it was absolutely superb to see George again and shake the hand of a football legend.

I would like to find a Kevin Beattie and it is my ambition to find a player who will go out and play for England. It is great to be involved with a football club again and I know that I can be an asset. There are a lot of people working for clubs who have never played the great game and that annoys me. How the hell they can get into clubs is a total mystery to me. I suppose it must be a bit of arse-licking that gets them there, but maybe that's my problem as I don't kiss arses.

1998 was the twentieth anniversary of our great F.A. Cup win in 1978 against the mighty Arsenal. The local newspaper, the Evening Star, with Ipswich Borough Council, Ipswich Town Football Club sponsored a gala evening at the Ipswich Corn Exchange and Town Hall. We rode on an open top bus through the town and the club borrowed the F.A. Cup for the day so we could parade it and show it off to the fans again. It was wonderful to be on the balcony and see their faces and it brought back a lot of memories for me and all the other players.

I still go down to Portman Road and watch the Town play and get a great buzz from seeing the fans and being asked for autographs. They all ask how I am getting on and have I got my boots in the back of the car just in case. That makes me feel good. The Town supporters never forget the players from the past who have come through the youth team into the first team.

The only thing I don't like about watching is having to sit there and know there is nothing I can do to help the team and by the time the game ends I feel I have played ninety minutes myself. I am sure I am speaking on behalf of all ex-players by

154

saying, many thanks for looking after us and making us feel welcome.

Luckily, I am also now involved in a weekly column with the Evening Star, talking about football in general. This really keeps my mind active and thoughts back on the game. The column is written by my old mate Mel Henderson, who does an absolutely superb job in writing up my comments, and I hope this may help in getting more media work in the future and to relaunch myself back into the public eye.

One very special person I would like to thank is Pat Godbold. She has been with the club for many, many years. She has been secretary to, I think, about seven managers and without Pat I think the place might not have run the way it has. She makes you very welcome and arranges ex-players reunion dinners every year and she always has a smile on her face for us. Thanks for all your help Pat, it is greatly appreciated.

I think George Burley and the present staff and chairman have done a great job and they have bought some good players and some youth players through the system. I think today they have a good side for the future and hopefully it will not be too long before they are back in the Premiership.

Ipswich Town is in my blood, it is a part of me and my life. I love the town, the supporters and the people of Suffolk and I hope that one day I see them playing in the Premiership and back in Europe, just as I had the privilege to do all those years ago.

25

My record at Ipswich

During the period from August 1972 and April 1981, I made a total of 296 appearances for Ipswich Town, and another 11 as substitute and I scored a total of 32 goals.

1972-73 Season

Division One:	37 games + 1 sub	5 goals
F.A. Cup:	1 game	
Football League Cup:	2 games	
Texaco Cup:	8 games	

DIVISION ONE

Date	Opponent		Result	Score	Goals
Aug 12	Manchester United	A	won	2-1	
Aug 15	Norwich City	H	lost	1-2	
Aug 23	Leeds United	A	drew	3-3	1 goal
Aug 26	Newcastle United	A	won	2-1	
Aug 29	Sheffield United	A	drew	0-0	
Sept 2	Tottenham Hotspur	H	drew	1-1	
Sept 9	Southampton	A	won	2-1	
Sept 23	Chelsea	A	lost	0-2	
	(as substitute for Ian Collard)				
Sept 30	Leicester City	H	lost	0-2	
Oct 7	West Ham United	H	drew	1-1	
Oct 14	Arsenal	A	lost	0-1	
Oct 21	Derby County	H	won	3-1	1 goal
Oct 28	Everton	A	drew	2-2	
Nov 4	Leeds United	H	drew	2-2	
Nov 11	Norwich City	A	drew	0-0	
Nov 18	Wolverhampton Wand.	A	won	1-0	
Dec 2	Manchester City	A	drew	1-1	
Dec 5	Coventry City	H	won	2-0	

Dec 9	Crystal Palace	H	won	2-1	
Dec 16	Liverpool	H	drew	1-1	
Dec 23	West Bromwich Albion	A	lost	0-2	
Dec 26	Chelsea	H	won	3-0	1 goal
Dec 30	Birmingham City	A	lost	1-2	
Jan 6	Newcastle United	H	won	1-0	
Jan 20	Tottenham Hotspur	A	won	1-0	
Jan 27	Southampton	H	drew	2-2	
Feb 17	Manchester United	H	won	4-1	
Mar 2	West Ham United	A	won	1-0	
Mar 10	Arsenal	H	lost	1-2	
Mar 17	West Bromwich Albion	H	won	2-0	1 goal
Mar 24	Everton	H	lost	0-1	
Mar 31	Coventry City	A	lost	1-2	1 goal
Apr 4	Stoke City	A	lost	0-1	
Apr 7	Manchester City	H	drew	1-1	
Apr 21	Wolverhampton Wand.	H	won	2-1	
Apr 24	Leicester City	A	drew	1-1	
Apr 28	Sheffield United	H	drew	1-1	
Apr 30	Derby County	A	lost	0-3	

F.A. CUP

Feb 3	Chelsea	A	lost	0-2

FOOTBALL LEAGUE CUP

Sept 5	Newport County	A	won	3-0
Oct 3	Stoke City	H	lost	1-2

TEXACO CUP

Sept 12	St Johnstone	H	won	4-2
Sept 27	St Johnstone	A	won	2-0
Oct 24	Wolverhampton Wand.	H	won	2-1
Nov 7	Wolverhampton Wand.	A	won	1-0
Mar 14	Newcastle United	A	drew	1-1
Apr 10	Newcastle United	H	won	1-0
May 4	Norwich City	H	won	2-1
May 7	Norwich City	A	won	2-1

(Texaco Cup Final won 4-2 on aggregate)

157

1973-74 Season

Division One:	42 games		2 goals
F.A. Cup:	3 games		3 goals
Football League Cup:	4 games		
UEFA Cup:	8 games		1 goal

DIVISION ONE

Aug 25	Leicester City	H	drew	1-1	
Aug 27	West Ham United	A	drew	3-3	
Sept 1	Everton	A	lost	0-3	
Sept 4	Newcastle United	H	lost	1-3	
Sept 8	Manchester United	H	won	2-1	
Sept 12	Newcastle United	A	lost	1-3	
Sept 15	Stoke City	A	drew	1-1	
Sept 22	Burnley	H	won	3-2	
Sept 29	Birmingham City	A	won	3-0	
Oct 6	Tottenham Hotspur	H	drew	0-0	
Oct 13	Chelsea	A	won	3-2	
Oct 20	Arsenal	A	drew	0-0	
Oct 27	Wolverhampton Wand.	H	won	2-0	
Nov 3	Coventry City	A	won	1-0	
Nov 10	Derby County	H	won	3-0	1 goal
Nov 17	Liverpool	A	lost	2-4	
Nov 24	Manchester City	H	won	2-1	
Dec 8	Leeds United	H	lost	0-3	
Dec 15	Southampton	A	lost	0-2	
Dec 22	Birmingham City	H	won	3-0	
Dec 26	Norwich City	A	won	2-1	
Dec 29	Manchester United	A	lost	0-2	
Jan 1	Everton	H	won	3-0	
Jan 12	Stoke City	H	drew	1-1	
Jan 19	Leicester City	A	lost	0-5	
Feb 2	Southampton	H	won	7-0	1 goal
Feb 5	West Ham United	H	lost	1-3	
Feb 9	Burnley	A	won	1-0	
Feb 23	Tottenham Hotspur	A	drew	1-1	
Feb 26	Chelsea	H	drew	1-1	
Mar 2	Norwich City	H	drew	1-1	

Mar 9	Wolverhampton Wand.	A	lost	1-3
Mar 12	Sheffield United	A	won	3-0
Mar 16	Arsenal	H	drew	2-2
Mar 23	Derby County	A	lost	0-2
Mar 30	Coventry City	H	won	3-0
Apr 6	Manchester City	A	won	3-1
Apr 12	Queens Park Rangers	A	won	1-0
Apr 13	Liverpool	H	drew	1-1
Apr 15	Queens Park Rangers	H	won	1-0
Apr 20	Leeds United	A	lost	2-3
Apr 27	Sheffield United	H	lost	0-1

F.A. CUP

Jan 5	Sheffield United	H	won	3-2	2 goals
Jan 26	Manchester United	A	won	1-0	1 goal
Feb 16	Liverpool	A	lost	0-2	

FOOTBALL LEAGUE CUP

Oct 8	Leeds United	H	won	2-0
Oct 31	Fulham	A	drew	2-2
Nov 14	Fulham	H	won	2-1
Nov 21	Birmingham City	H	lost	1-3

UEFA CUP

Sept 19	Real Madrid	H	won	1-0	
Oct 3	Real Madrid	A	drew	0-0	
Oct 24	Lazio	H	won	4-0	
Nov 7	Lazio	A	lost	2-4	
Nov 28	FC Twente	H	won	1-0	
Dec 12	FC Twente	A	won	2-1	
Mar 6	Lokomotiv Leipzig	H	won	1-0	1 goal
Mar 20	Lokomotiv Leipzig	A	lost	0-1	

(lost on penalties)

1974-75 Season

Division One:	37 games		6 goals
F.A. Cup:	8 games		
Football League Cup:	5 games		
UEFA Cup:	2 games		

DIVISION ONE

Date	Opponent	H/A	Result	Score	Goals
Aug 17	Tottenham Hotspur	A	won	1-0	
Aug 20	Arsenal	A	won	1-0	
Aug 24	Burnley	H	won	2-0	
Aug 27	Arsenal	H	won	3-0	1 goal
Aug 31	Sheffield United	A	lost	1-3	
Sept 7	Everton	H	won	1-0	
Sept 14	Luton Town	A	won	4-1	
Sept 21	Chelsea	H	won	2-0	
Sept 24	Stoke City	H	won	3-1	
Sept 28	Newcastle United	A	lost	0-1	
Oct 5	Queens Park Rangers	A	lost	0-1	
Oct 12	Leeds United	H	drew	0-0	
Oct 15	Burnley	A	lost	0-1	
Oct 19	West Ham United	A	lost	0-1	
Oct 26	Manchester City	H	drew	1-1	
Nov 2	Liverpool	H	won	1-0	
Nov 9	Wolverhampton Wand.	A	lost	1-2	
Nov 16	Coventry City	H	won	4-0	
Nov 30	Carlisle United	H	won	3-1	
Dec 7	Middlesbrough	A	lost	0-3	
Dec 14	Tottenham Hotspur	H	won	4-0	1 goal
Dec 26	Luton Town	H	lost	0-1	
Jan 11	Middlesbrough	H	won	2-0	
Jan 18	Carlisle United	A	won	2-1	
Feb 1	Wolverhampton Wand.	H	won	2-0	1 goal
Feb 8	Liverpool	A	lost	2-5	1 goal
Feb 22	Coventry City	A	lost	1-3	
Feb 25	Derby County	H	won	3-0	1 goal
Mar 1	Sheffield United	H	lost	0-1	
Mar 15	Newcastle United	H	won	5-4	
Mar 18	Stoke City	A	won	2-1	

Mar 22	Everton	A	drew	1-1
Apr 1	Birmingham City	H	won	3-2
Apr 12	Queens Park Rangers	H	won	2-1
Apr 19	Leeds United	A	lost	1-2
Apr 23	Manchester City	A	drew	1-1
Apr 26	West Ham United	H	won	4-1	1 goal

F.A. CUP

Jan 4	Wolverhampton Wand.	A	won	2-1
Jan 25	Liverpool	H	won	1-0
Feb 15	Aston Villa	H	won	3-2
Mar 8	Leeds United	H	drew	0-0
Mar 11	Leeds United	A	drew	1-1
Mar 25	Leeds United	-	drew	0-0

(match played at Filbert Street, Leicester)

Apr 5	West Ham United	-	drew	0-0

(match played at Villa Park)

Apr 9	West Ham United	-	lost	1-2

(match played at Stamford Bridge)

FOOTBALL LEAGUE CUP

Sept 10	Coventry City	A	won	2-1
Oct 8	Hereford United	H	won	4-1
Nov 12	Stoke City	H	won	2-1
Dec 4	Norwich City	A	drew	1-1
Dec 10	Norwich City	H	lost	1-2

UEFA CUP

Sept 18	FC Twente	H	drew	2-2
Oct 2	FC Twente	A	drew	1-1

(lost on away goals)

1975-76 Season

Division One:	29 games		4 goals
F.A. Cup:	3 games		
Football League Cup:	1 game		
UEFA Cup:	3 games		

DIVISION ONE

Date	Opponent	H/A	Result	Score	Goals
Aug 16	Newcastle United	H	lost	0-3	
Aug 20	Tottenham Hotspur	A	drew	1-1	
Aug 23	Leeds United	A	lost	0-1	
Aug 26	Burnley	H	drew	0-0	
Aug 30	Birmingham City	H	won	4-2	
Sept 6	Coventry City	A	drew	0-0	
Sept 20	Manchester United	A	lost	0-1	
Sept 23	Norwich City	H	won	2-0	1 goal
Sept 27	Middlesbrough	H	lost	0-3	
Oct 11	Stoke City	A	lost	0-1	
Oct 18	Leicester City	H	drew	1-1	
Oct 25	Manchester City	A	drew	1-1	
Nov 8	Wolverhampton Wand.	A	lost	0-1	
Nov 15	Queens Park Rangers	H	drew	1-1	
Nov 22	Leicester City	A	drew	0-0	
Nov 29	Sheffield United	H	drew	1-1	
Dec 6	Everton	A	drew	3-3	
Dec 13	Leeds United	H	won	2-1	
Dec 20	Newcastle United	A	drew	1-1	
Dec 26	Arsenal	H	won	2-0	
Dec 27	West Ham United	A	won	2-1	
Jan 10	Liverpool	A	drew	3-3	
Jan 17	Coventry City	H	drew	1-1	
Jan 31	Tottenham Hotspur	H	lost	1-2	
Feb 7	Burnley	A	won	1-0	1 goal
Feb 17	Wolverhampton Wand.	H	won	3-0	2 goals
Feb 21	Queens Park Rangers	A	lost	1-3	
Mar 20	Sheffield United	A	won	2-1	
Apr 7	Manchester City	H	won	2-1	

F.A. CUP

Jan 3	Halifax Town	H	won	3-1
Jan 24	Wolverhampton Wand.	H	drew	0-0
Jan 27	Wolverhampton Wand.	A	lost	0-1

FOOTBALL LEAGUE CUP

Sept 9	Leeds United	A	lost	2-3

UEFA CUP

Sept 17	Feyenoord	A	won	2-1
Oct 1	Feyenoord	H	won	2-0
Oct 22	FC Bruges	H	won	3-0

1976-77 Season

Division One:	30 games + 1 sub	5 goals
F.A. Cup:	2 games	
Football League Cup:	2 games	

DIVISION ONE

Aug 21	Tottenham Hotspur	H	won	3-1	
Aug 24	Everton	A	drew	1-1	1 goal
Aug 28	Queens Park Rangers	H	drew	2-2	1 goal
Sept 4	Aston Villa	A	lost	2-5	
Sept 11	Leicester City	H	drew	0-0	
Sept 25	Arsenal	H	won	3-1	1 goal
Oct 2	Bristol City	A	won	2-1	
Oct 16	West Ham United	A	won	2-0	
Oct 23	Manchester City	H	won	1-0	
Oct 30	Manchester United	A	won	1-0	
Nov 6	West Bromwich Albion	H	won	7-0	1 goal
Nov 20	Leeds United	H	drew	1-1	
Nov 23	Sunderland	H	won	3-1	1 goal
Nov 27	Middlesbrough	A	won	2-0	
Dec 4	Liverpool	H	won	1-0	
Dec 7	Birmingham City	A	won	4-2	
Dec 18	Derby County	H	drew	0-0	
Dec 27	Coventry City	A	drew	1-1	

Jan 3	Manchester United	H	won	2-1
Jan 15	Everton	H	won	2-0
Jan 22	Tottenham Hotspur	A	lost	0-1
Feb 12	Aston Villa	H	won	1-0
Feb 15	Norwich City	H	won	5-0
Feb 19	Leicester City	A	lost	0-1
Feb 26	Stoke City	H	lost	0-1
Mar 5	Arsenal	A	won	4-1
Mar 9	Newcastle United	A	drew	1-1
Mar 19	Sunderland	A	lost	0-1
	(as substitute for Keith Bertschin)			
Apr 2	Manchester City	A	lost	1-2
Apr 5	Coventry City	H	won	2-1
Apr 9	Norwich City	A	won	1-0

F.A. CUP

Jan 8	Bristol City	H	won	4-1

FOOTBALL LEAGUE CUP

Aug 31	Brighton & H. Albion	H	drew	0-0
Sept 7	Brighton & H. Albion	A	lost	1-2

1977-78 Season

Division One:	14 games
F.A. Cup:	3 games
Football League Cup:	1 game
UEFA Cup:	3 games

DIVISION ONE

Aug 20	Arsenal	H	won	1-0
Aug 24	Derby County	A	drew	0-0
Aug 27	Manchester United	A	drew	0-0
Sept 17	Liverpool	H	drew	1-1
Sept 24	Middlesbrough	A	drew	1-1
Oct 1	Newcastle United	H	won	2-1
Oct 4	Nottingham Forest	A	lost	0-4
Oct 8	West Bromwich Albion	A	lost	0-1

Mar 18	Coventry City	H	drew	1-1
Mar 21	Middlesbrough	H	drew	1-1
Mar 24	West Ham United	A	lost	0-3
Mar 25	Queens Park Rangers	A	drew	3-3
Mar 27	Norwich City	H	won	4-0
Apr 11	Birmingham City	A	drew	0-0

F.A. CUP

Jan 28	Hartlepool United	H	won	4-1
Apr 8	West Bromwich Albion	-	won	3-1
	(played at Highbury)			
May 6	Arsenal	-	won	1-0
	(played at Wembley)			

FOOTBALL LEAGUE CUP

Aug 30	Northampton Town	H	won	5-0

UEFA CUP

Sept 14	Landskrona Bois	A	won	1-0
Sept 28	Landskrona Bois	H	won	5-0
Nov 23	Barcelona	H	won	3-0

1978-79 Season

Division One:	19 games + 1 sub	1 goal
F.A. Cup:	3 games	1 goal
Football League Cup:	1 game	
E. Cup Winners Cup:	3 games	

DIVISION ONE

Aug 26	Manchester United	H	won	3-0
Sept 2	Middlesbrough	A	drew	0-0
Sept 9	Aston Villa	H	lost	0-2
Sept 16	Wolverhampton Wand.	A	won	3-1
Sept 23	Bristol City	H	lost	0-1
Sept 30	Southampton	A	won	2-1
Oct 7	Coventry City	A	drew	2-2
Nov 11	West Bromwich Albion	H	lost	0-1

Nov 18	Manchester United	A	lost	0-2	
Nov 21	Middlesbrough	H	won	2-1	
Nov 25	Manchester City	A	won	2-1	
Dec 2	Leeds United	H	lost	2-3	1 goal
Jan 20	Wolverhampton Wand.	H	won	3-1	
Feb 10	Southampton	H	drew	0-0	
Feb 24	Everton	A	won	1-0	
Mar 31	Manchester City	H	won	2-1	
Apr 3	Birmingham City	A	drew	1-1	
Apr 7	Leeds United	A	drew	1-1	
Apr 14	Norwich City	A	won	1-0	
May 11	Queens Park Rangers	A	won	4-0	

(as substitute for Clive Woods)

F.A. CUP

Jan 10	Carlisle United	H	won	3-2	1 goal
Jan 27	Orient	A	drew	0-0	
Feb 26	Bristol Rovers	H	won	6-1	

FOOTBALL LEAGUE CUP

| Aug 30 | Blackpool | A | lost | 0-2 |

EUROPEAN CUP WINNERS CUP

Sept 13	AZ 67 Alkmaar	A	drew	0-0
Sept 27	AZ 67 Alkmaar	H	won	2-0
Mar 21	Barcelona	A	lost	0-1

1979-80 Season

Division One:	10 games	
F.A. Cup:	2 games as substitute	1 goal
UEFA Cup:	2 games	1 goal

DIVISION ONE

Oct 27	Middlesbrough	H	won	1-0
Nov 3	Nottingham Forest	A	lost	0-2
Nov 10	Aston Villa	H	drew	0-0
Nov 24	Southampton	H	won	3-1

Dec 1	Coventry City	A	lost	1-4	
Dec 8	Manchester City	H	won	4-0	
Feb 9	Everton	A	won	4-0	
Mar 1	Manchester United	H	won	6-0	
Mar 11	Middlesbrough	A	drew	1-1	
Mar 29	Derby County	H	drew	1-1	

F.A. CUP

Jan 5	Preston North End	A	won	3-0	
	(as substitute for John Wark)				
Mar 8	Everton	A	lost	1-2	1 goal
	(as substitute for John Wark)				

UEFA CUP

Oct 24	Grasshoppers Zurich	A	drew	0-0	
Nov 7	Grasshoppers Zurich	H	drew	1-1	1 goal
	(lost on away goals)				

1980-81 Season

Division One:	7 games		1 goal
F.A. Cup:	2 games		
UEFA Cup:	2 games + 6 as sub.		1 goal

DIVISION ONE

Sept 13	Crystal Palace	A	won	2-1	
Oct 25	Sunderland	A	won	2-0	
Nov 8	Southampton	A	drew	3-3	
Feb 7	Crystal Palace	H	won	3-2	
Feb 17	Middlesbrough	H	won	1-0	
Feb 21	Wolverhampton Wand.	H	won	3-1	1 goal
Feb 28	Coventry City	A	won	4-0	

F.A. CUP

Feb 14	Charlton Athletic	H	won	2-0	
Apr 11	Manchester City	-	lost	0-1	
	(match played at Villa Park)				

167

UEFA CUP

Sept 17	Aris Salonika	H	won	5-1	
	(as substitute for Arnold Mühren)				
Oct 1	Aris Salonika	A	lost	1-3	
	(as substitute for Arnold Mühren)				
Oct 22	Bohemians, Prague	H	won	3-0	1 goal
	(as substitute for John Wark)				
Nov 5	Bohemians, Prague	A	lost	0-2	
Nov 26	Widzew Lodz	H	won	5-0	
	(as substitute for Mick Mills)				
Dec 10	Widzew Lodz	A	lost	0-1	
	(as substitute for Arnold Mühren)				
Mar 4	St Etienne	A	won	4-1	
Apr 8	1FC Cologne	H	won	1-0	
	(as substitute for Steve McCall)				